Stories from Lake Wobegon

Advanced Listening and Conversation Skills

Frances Boyd

David Quinn

Monologues by Garrison Keillor

Longman

New York & London

Stories from Lake Wobegon: Advanced Listening and Conversation Skills

Longman, 95 Church Street, White Plains, N.Y. 10601

Associated companies:
Longman Group Ltd., London
Longman Cheshire Pty., Melbourne
Longman Paul Pty., Auckland
Copp Clark Pitman, Toronto

Chapter 1, Ex. 9: Keillor, Garrison, *We Are Still Married*, New York: Viking Press, 1989,
pp. 138–139.
Chapter 5, Ex. 9: Dorsens, Richard M., *Folktales Told Around the World*, Chicago:
University of Chicago Press, 1975.
Chapter 8, Ex. 9: Forbes, Malcom, "How to Write a Business Letter" in *How to Use the
Power of the Written Word*, Billings S. Fress, Jr., ed., New York: Anchor-Doubleday, 1985,
pp. 2–3.
Chapter 10, Ex. 9: Didion, Joan, *Slouching toward Bethlehem*, New York: Simon and
Schuster, 1961, pp. 133, 134, 136.

The stories appearing on the accompanying cassette tape are copyrighted by Garrison Keillor,
and the names and the characters and the stories are the intellectual property of Garrison
Keillor. All rights are reserved.

The "News from Lake Wobegon" stories were first heard on the live radio broadcasts of
Garrison Keillor's "A Prairie Home Companion," which was produced by Minnesota Public
Radio and is still heard on public radio stations across the country.

For further information on stations carrying the program and broadcast times, or on related
products such as books or recordings, write Minnesota Public Radio, 45 East Seventh Street,
St. Paul, Minnesota 55101.

Distributed in the United Kingdom by Longman Group
Ltd., Longman House, Burnt Mill, Harlow, Essex CM20
2JE, England, and by associated companies, branches,
and representatives throughout the world.

Executive editor: Joanne Dresner
Development editors: Karen Davy and Penny Laporte
Production editor: Helen B. Ambrosio
Text design: The Quarasan Group, Inc.
Cover design: Joseph DePinho
Cover illustration: Mike Lynch
Text art: George Chiang and The Quarasan Group, Inc.
Production supervisor: Kathleen M. Ryan

Library of Congress Cataloging in Publication Data

Boyd, Frances Armstrong.
   Stories from Lake Wobegon : advanced listening and conversation
skills / by Frances Boyd, David Quinn : monologues by Garrison Keillor.
    p.   cm.
  ISBN 0-8013-0312-5
  1. Readers—Lake Wobegon (Imaginary place) 2. English language—
Textbooks for foreign speakers. 3. Lake Wobegon (Imaginary place)—
Fiction. 4. Conversation. 5. Listening. I. Quinn, David, 1953–
II. Keillor, Garrison. III. Title.
PE1127.L6B6 1990
428.3′4—dc20   89-49356
                                          CIP

ABCDEFGHIJ-HC-99 98 97 96 95 94 93 92 91 90

Contents

Acknowledgments

This book has become a reality thanks to James Day at *Publivision, Inc.*; Ilene Zatal at *A Prairie Home Companion*; Donna Avery at *Minnesota Public Radio*; Jennifer Howe and Garrison Keillor at the *American Humor Institute*; Gertrude Moskowitz for inspiration on the form of our Telling Your Own Stories exercises; Karen Davy, Joanne Dresner, Arley Gray, Penny Laporte and Steve Soltow at *Longman*; friends Martee Levi and Ulla Skaerved; friend and artist George Chiang; and our colleagues at the *American Language Program*, especially Patrick Aquilina, Karen Brockmann, Sheri Handel, Mary Jerome, Jane Kenefick, Louis Levi, Carol Numrich and Janice Sartori.

To Lucy Carlborg Rosborough and Peggy Montgomery for tuning us in.
To Carlos Velazquez and Leslie Quinn for keeping us going.
To our students for telling their own stories.

Preface

It's very hard for intelligent persons like us to accept being as stupid as we are in another language. It's frustrating, like becoming a child and still remembering how it was to be an adult. Like trying to play Mozart on a beer bottle. You know what you want to say and it won't come out.

A few years ago I fell in love with a European woman, a Dane, and after a long walk with her by the river, I drove to a library and got a book called *Teach Yourself Danish* and sat down that evening and tried to learn a lot in a couple of hours. I learned a few phrases including *hvad hedder dette pa dansk* (What is that called in Danish?) and *jeg elsker dig* (I love you) and *undskyld* (Excuse me). Like most Americans, I thought I could learn another language pretty easily. When I went to Denmark to visit her, I knew Danish well enough to be able to say things like, "Good day, my esteemed sausage, it is a pleasure to make the acquaintance of your suitcase and to thank your delightful wife for spending the night with me." They replied, in perfect English: "Your Danish is very good. Where in America are you from?" Over there, I can't be as humorous or romantic or brave or smart as I can be in my own language. Usually I'm a real blockhead.

Since I married her and became an exchange husband, I have learned how hard it is to live in a different culture and speak a new language. We like to think we are tolerant but down deep we find it strange and unpleasant that other people are not like us. My hometown of Lake Wobegon is full of men and women who aren't tolerant at all and who look at strangers and foreigners as *aliens*, dangerous people with wrong ideas about life. If you are from Vietnam or the Soviet Union or Mexico or some other country, you might find it very hard to live in Lake Wobegon. So it's good that you should listen to these stories and know more about the people who don't know much about you and learn to laugh at them. If you can laugh at Americans, the way we Americans do, you'll get along pretty well.

Garrison Keillor

To the Student

Stories from Lake Wobegon is a high-intermediate to advanced listening and speaking program. Young adult and adult students of English will enjoy hearing the humorous monologues of Garrison Keillor, as listening and speaking skills are strengthened through the text's vocabulary, comprehension, interpretation and storytelling activities.

Each of the twelve units contains the following types of exercises. Here are some suggestions for completing each activity.

Judging from Experience: You are asked to look at a drawing. In order to answer the questions, you have to rely on your own experience, and make educated guesses. This activity helps get you ready to listen to the story, and should not take more than two or three minutes.

Vocabulary: Depending on the length of the story, each story is divided into two or three parts. Before you listen to each part, you will do one or more vocabulary exercises which will help you understand the story. In these exercises, you must discover the meaning of the vocabulary items. The rest of the sentence will usually help you guess the meaning of the new word.

Getting the Gist of the Story: You will read one or more questions and then listen to the first part of the story. If you can answer these questions, you have understood the gist, or the main idea, of the story. Spend no more than a minute or two comparing your answers with those of classmates.

Listening for Detail: In the previous exercise, you listened for the "gist." Now, you will hear the same part of the story again, but this time you have to listen very carefully in order to hear detailed information. Before starting the tape, read the questions. Then choose the correct answer as you listen.

Predicting and Listening: You are asked to think about what might happen next in the story. Later you will hear how Garrison finishes the story, but you can have some fun using your imagination first. Take about five minutes for this. Then listen to the rest of the story and compare your predictions with the ending you heard.

Getting the Joke: You will think and talk about the parts of the story where Garrison's audience laughs. Some of the jokes are funny because they are an exaggeration, or an overstatement. Others are funny because they are an understatement. Or the situation may be ironic because of the personalities of the people involved or because of the social situation they are in. Plan to listen to the tape on another day, since Garrison's stories get better every time you listen. As one student said, "I really feel I have understood if I can laugh with the audience." Spend 20 minutes or so on this exercise.

Reviewing Vocabulary: You will review vocabulary that will prepare you for Retelling the Story, an exercise that comes later in the unit. If you want, you can review the earlier vocabulary exercises before doing this one. Some teachers and students prefer to do this exercise at home.

Interpreting the Characters: Here, you have a chance to talk about the personalities and the motivations of the people in the story. The characters in Garrison's stories are interesting people, and it is fun to think about why they do what they do. You may want to spend 15 to 20 minutes on this exercise.

Retelling the Story: This is a speaking exercise. Try to include as many details as possible, since details are what make the story funny and what make the characters come alive. Challenge each other to remember more details than those given. Some classes like to spend more than half an hour on this activity.

Telling Your Own Stories: This is one of the most important exercises in the book, because it gives you a chance to tell your classmates a story from your own experience. It is not necessary to try to be funny. What is important is that you tell a story about something that really happened to you or to someone you know. Garrison's stories are windows into the life of Americans living in Lake Wobegon. Your stories are windows into the life and the people of your country. We are sure that the other students in your class will enjoy looking in.

Getting into the Language: Here, we take a piece of the language used in the story and point out something interesting about it. It might be a grammatical structure or a special way in which the language is used. We give you examples and explanations, and then ask you to practice the structure. Many teachers and students prefer to do this exercise for homework.

Extending the Story in Writing: In this exercise, you have a choice of writing assignments. You can write down a story that a classmate has told or write down your own story. Each unit also has a special writing task, such as an essay, a letter or a news item. In these writing assignments, you will be asked to use the vocabulary and structures from the unit. Many classes prefer to do this exercise for homework.

Tapescript: It is important to notice that these are exact transcripts of spoken language, which can be very different from written language. The occasional incomplete sentences and grammatical "mistakes" that you hear are normal in spoken language.

Answer Key: Included here are answers to exercise items that have only one best answer.

Introducing Lake Wobegon

The stories in this book all take place in or around Lake Wobegon, Minnesota, an imaginary rural village in the midwestern part of the United States. According to its creator, Garrison Keillor, it is "a town that time forgot and the decades cannot improve." Although Lake Wobegon does not really exist, the concerns of the people who live there seem very familiar to most Americans.

For more than twelve years, Mr. Keillor was the host of a weekly radio program called "A Prairie Home Companion." The show consisted mainly of live music, advertisements for imaginary products and humorous monologues. The twelve stories you will hear as you study this book were told to a live audience and broadcast all over the United States as part of this Saturday evening radio program.

UNIT 1
The Living Flag

1 | *Judging from Experience*

Read the questions. Discuss the answers with your classmates.

1. Look at the drawing. What are these people doing? Why?
2. How do you feel about participating in events like this?
3. Look at the title. What do you think this story is about?

Part One

A | *Vocabulary*

Read the sentences and find the word or expression in the box that means the same as the *italicized* words. Then compare your answers with those of a classmate. If you disagree, consult another classmate, a dictionary or your teacher.

1. __C__ Flag Day is a holiday that *is observed* in June.

2. _____ The largest urban area in the state of Minnesota is *the Cities*, or *the Twin Cities*.

3. _____ On Flag Day, people often *stop by* their local stores to buy flags.

4. _____ Baseball players usually wear colored *caps* on their heads.

5. _____ If all the food is eaten at a meal, there is nothing *leftover*.

6. _____ The professor explained the equation several times, but the student still could not *see* how it worked.

7. _____ It *is patriotic* to display a flag on a national holiday.

8. _____ When soldiers stand or move together, they are supposed to stay in straight lines. Nobody should *break ranks*.

9. _____ My friend's note says that she will *be right back*. But I have been waiting half an hour, and she is still not here.

a) shows love of one's country
b) remaining
c) is celebrated
d) return soon
e) leave the line
f) Minneapolis and St. Paul
g) visit
h) understand
i) hats

B | *Getting the Gist of the Story*

This is a story about Flag Day, June 14th, an American holiday that celebrates the selection of the official United States flag in 1777. Although the holiday is often marked on calendars, few people actually observe it. In this story, Hjalmar Ingqvist, a citizen of Lake Wobegon, participates in an unusual Flag Day celebration.

Listen to Part One of the story. Read the question and write your answer. Then compare your answer with those of your classmates.

What is a living flag?

C Listening for Detail

Listen again to Part One. Circle the letter of the answer that best completes each sentence. Then compare your answers with those of a classmate. Listen again if you disagree with each other.

1. It is possible that Flag Day is not observed

   a) in Lake Wobegon.

   b) in the Cities.

   c) by the Chamber of Commerce.

2. To observe Flag Day now, people in Lake Wobegon

   a) have large celebrations.

   b) go to the Cities.

   c) fly flags.

3. In 1936, the living flag was formed with

   a) about 400 flags.

   b) approximately 400 citizens.

   c) everyone who lived in town.

4. Hjalmar Ingqvist was responsible for

   a) organizing the living flag.

   b) selling the caps.

   c) giving out flags.

5. One person left the living flag because he or she

   a) was tired.

   b) had to go home.

   c) wanted to see the whole flag.

6. The person who ran up to the roof of the Central Building said that everyone

   a) had to go home.

   b) should look at the flag.

   c) was patriotic.

Part Two

D Vocabulary

Circle the letter of the expression that is closest in meaning to the *italicized* word or phrase. Then compare your answers with those of a classmate.

1. The flag was unusual. Even though it was getting late, everybody wanted to *have a look.*

   a) remember it   **b)** see it briefly   **c)** study it

2. After they had been standing in the flag formation for several hours, some people said, "OK, *that's it* now. We can go home."

   a) we've been doing this long enough   **b)** that's right   **c)** it's your turn

3. Other people who were waiting to see the unusual flag said, "Hey, *hold on* now. We didn't get a chance to see it yet."

   a) continue   **b)** stand by the railing   **c)** wait

4. It seemed that everybody wanted to see the flag. After several hours of standing on Main Street, *tempers were running short.*

   a) people were getting angry and impatient   **b)** people began to run

   c) people did not have a lot of time

5. In many religions, people *kneel* when they pray.

   a) sit down   **b)** rest on their knees   **c)** stand up

6. Mrs. Quigley, one of the last people in line, was moving slowly. She was told to "go have a look at the flag, and *make it quick.*"

   a) hurry up   **b)** be careful   **c)** go by yourself

7. Mrs. Quigley did not want to keep people waiting while she looked at the flag. She said, "I don't want you to *go to any trouble.*"

   a) make any trouble   **b)** make a special effort   **c)** get into trouble

8. She insisted, "Don't do anything special *on my account.* I have seen flags before."

   a) for the event   **b)** for the account   **c)** for me

9. Which is the *lower right-hand* corner of the flag?

   a)    b)    c)

10. Because they did not want to wait any longer, some of the townspeople *hustled* Mrs. Quigley up the stairs.

    a) followed   **b)** hurried   **c)** carried

11. When one woman *leaned* back to see the top of the Central Building, her cap fell off.

    a) looked   **b)** stepped   **c)** bent

$\boxed{E}$ *Predicting and Listening*

1 Working in small groups, discuss the question. Predict what might happen next in the story. Write down at least two possible answers.

How will it be possible for everyone in the living flag to see it?

a. _____

b. _____

c. _____

2 Keeping your same groups, listen to the end of the story. Discuss how your predictions were different from the ending you heard.

$\boxed{F}$ *Listening for Detail*

Listen again to Part Two. Circle the letter of the answer that best completes each sentence. Then compare your answers with those of a classmate. Listen again if you disagree with each other.

1. After a few hours, people who had not seen the flag yet wanted to

    a) go home.

    b) have a chance to see it.

    c) sit down.

2. Mrs. Quigley said that she

    a) would hurry up.

    b) did not need to have a look.

    c) had never seen such a beautiful flag.

3. Many people helped Mrs. Quigley up to the roof because they

    a) liked her.

    b) were worried about her.

    c) were impatient.

3 Getting the Joke

Read each item and decide which answer explains why the audience laughs. Circle your choice. Then, working in groups, compare your answers. If you agree, discuss the reasons for your choices. If you disagree, discuss your opinions and try to come to an agreement. In each case, there is one choice that best explains the joke.

1. "Oh, it's beautiful! You ought to see it. And then, of course, everybody had to have a look."
   Just like Hjalmar Ingqvist, the organizer of the living flag, one would expect participants to

   a) stay in their places in the flag.

   b) take photos.

   c) stand up all afternoon.

2. "And the living flag was becoming sort of a sitting, a kneeling flag."
   Because the flag is a patriotic symbol, one would expect participants in a living flag to be

   a) singing.

   b) standing proudly.

   c) sitting in chairs.

3. "And then, of course, somebody thought they would run home and get a camera."
   If participants in the living flag wait for this one person to get a camera, they will probably have to

   a) stand up again.

   b) leave early.

   c) wait for many people to go home to get their cameras.

4 Reviewing Vocabulary

Fill in each blank with one of these words or expressions. Be sure to use the correct form of the *italicized* words. Compare your answers with those of a classmate.

hustle	patriotic	that's it
hold on	*kneel*	*be* observed
make it quick	leftover	lean
lower right-hand	have a look	*cap*
tempers *run* short	*break* ranks	

Nowadays, Flag Day _____*is observed*_____ quietly in Lake Wobegon, but people used to do
₁

more. Back in 1936, Hjalmar Ingqvist bought 400 red, white and blue _____ from
₂

a traveling salesman. He thought it would be a _____ act if every citizen formed
₃

part of a living flag. Unfortunately, there were very few people _____ to
₄

appreciate it. As they all stood in the middle of town, somebody _____. After this
₅

person ran up onto the Central Building to _____, then everybody had to see the
₆

flag.

After several hours, people became impatient and _____. Citizens who had
₇

already seen the flag said, "OK, _____ now." But those who had not seen it yet
₈

said, "_____. We didn't get our chance!"
₉

By the time they got to the last person, Mrs. Quigley, most people were tired, so they

_____. They told her to _____. She refused to go, so the
₁₀ ₁₁

whole _____ corner of the flag grabbed her by the arms,
₁₂

_____ her up three flights of stairs to the roof and made her
₁₃

_____ out and look at the living flag.
₁₄

5 ## *Interpreting the Characters*

Read the following questions and answers. The answers are not mentioned directly in the story, but it is possible to make good guesses based on your knowledge of the story and of American life. Decide whether each answer is *likely* or *unlikely*. Circle your choice. Then, working in small groups, give reasons for your choices and discuss your opinions. There is no one correct answer, but there is more evidence for some choices than for others.

1. Why didn't Mrs. Quigley want to take a look at the living flag?

    a) It was a warm June day, and she wanted to go get a   *likely*   *unlikely*
        drink of iced tea.

    b) She did not want people to have to wait any longer   *likely*   *unlikely*
        just for her.

    c) She was afraid of heights and did not want to go up   *likely*   *unlikely*
        on the roof of the Central Building.

2. Why did the whole lower right-hand corner of the flag force Mrs. Quigley to have a look?

    a) They thought that she was not patriotic enough.   *likely*   *unlikely*

    b) They were impatient with her because she never   *likely*   *unlikely*
        wanted anyone to go to any trouble on her account.

    c) They wanted everyone to have a look because they   *likely*   *unlikely*
        planned to collect money from those who had seen
        the living flag to help pay for the caps.

6 ## *Retelling the Story*

Use these phrases to retell the story in your own words. As you speak, try to include as many details as you can. A different student may want to retell each part.

                                This information may help you:

Tomorrow is Flag Day in Lake Wobegon . . .   • Skoglund's store
                                          • fly flags
                                        • more before than now

In 1936, people in Lake Wobegon . . .

- a living flag
- traveling cap salesman
- Hjalmar Ingqvist
- Main Street
- somebody broke ranks and looked down

After one person had seen the flag, then . . .

- it took hours
- we can go home
- hold on now
- Mrs. Quigley
- hustled
- camera

7 | Telling Your Own Stories

1 Find out which classmates have had the following experiences. Ask yes/no questions: for example, "Have you ever participated in a patriotic parade?" Try to find one classmate for each statement. When you get a "yes" answer, write that classmate's name in the blank. Do not tell any stories yet. To begin the exercise, stand up and move around the classroom freely.

1. _____ has participated in a patriotic parade.
   (name)

2. _____ has been pressured by a salesperson to buy something
   (name)   unnecessary.

3. _____ has organized an event for more than 100 people.
   (name)

4. _____ has stood in line for a long time to see something.
   (name)

2 Look at your list above. If several of you have stories for each experience, one of you should volunteer to be the storyteller. You can tell your stories to the whole class or to small groups. If almost everyone has a story to tell, you might want to work in pairs and exchange stories.

8 Getting into the Language

A Notice the Structure: Causative Verbs

> The whole lower right-hand corner of that flag grabbed her and they hustled her up the stairs, and up on the roof of the Central Building, and they leaned her out, and they **made** her **look down** at the living flag.

Causative verbs *(get, make, have, let)* are used with other verbs to express the idea of persuading, allowing or causing someone else to do something. The causative verb can appear in any tense. When the second verb is active, use its simple, or base, form after *make, have* and *let;* use the *to* infinitive after *get*. When the second verb has a passive meaning, use the past participle. Study these examples.

Active Causative

get someone to do persuade	Hjalmar Ingqvist **got** a newspaper reporter **to photograph** the living flag.	He persuaded the reporter that this would be a newsworthy event.
make someone do force in a psychological or physical way	Hjalmar **did not make** the participants in the flag **stand up** until everyone had seen it.	He did not use his authority as the organizer to force the citizens to remain standing.
have someone do ask or pay	Next year the Mayor of Lake Wobegon **will have** the high school band **play** patriotic songs.	He plans to ask the high school for this service.
let someone do allow, permit	The Mayor **had never let** teenagers **climb up** on the roof of the Central Building before.	Before the living flag, he had never allowed them to go up on the roof.

Passive Causative

have/get something done Something is done because someone requested it or paid for it.	Several people who had taken pictures **had/got** their film **developed** the following week.	They took it to a photo shop and paid the shop to develop it for them.

B Practice the Structure

In the story, it was suggested that the idea for the living flag came from a traveling salesman. Imagine the conversation between Hjalmar Ingqvist and the salesman. Complete the conversation with the correct form of the verbs in parentheses, using either the active or passive form of the causative. Be sure to put the causative verb in an appropriate tense.

SALESMAN: _____*Let*_____ me _____*introduce*_____ you to a
                           (1. Let)   (2. introduce)
new patriotic way to celebrate Flag Day.

HJALMAR: Well, I guess so, but please _____ me
                                               (3. *negative*, make)
_____ anything. We're over our budget already.
(4. buy)

SALESMAN: The idea is to _____ the citizens
                                 (5. have)
_____ together to create a community
(6. work)
event. Listen to this: Lake Wobegon could have a living flag, a flag your citizens form themselves by standing in rows with red, white and blue caps on. It's a great way to build civic pride.

HJALMAR: _____ you _____ people
                                     (7. get)
in any other town _____ this before?
(8. do)

SALESMAN: Well, I was up in Bemidji just last week. The Mayor

_____ an article
(9. have)
_____ in the newspaper announcing the
(10. print)
plan. He _____ the Chamber of
(11. get)
Commerce _____ the caps as a public
(12. buy)
service. Everyone is excited about the plan.

HJALMAR: Sounds like a good idea. How far ahead do I need to order the caps?

SALESMAN: We _____ you _____ at
             (13. *negative*, make)   (14. wait)
all. If you tell me how many you need, I can

_____ your order _____
(15. have)   (16. process)
today and _____
(17. have)
it _____ next week.
(18. send)

9 | Extending the Story in Writing

A | Writing Down a Story

Write down a story from Exercise 7, either one you heard or your own. If you choose another student's story, show your work to the storyteller when you finish. Ask the storyteller to comment on your version. Then revise the story, making any necessary changes and corrections.

B | Writing a Personal Letter

Are you a letter writer? The personal letter is a special form of communication. Although many people prefer to pick up the telephone instead, those who write personal letters give the reader the joy of finding something in the mailbox, as well as the satisfaction of being able to read the words over and over.

Model

Here is part of a personal letter to Mrs. Quigley from her sister Ruth Temby, who lives in Fargo, a town in the neighboring state of North Dakota. These sisters have corresponded by letter every other week for many years.

> June 7, 1936
>
> Dear Mary,
>
> The squirrels have gathered around the kitchen door for breakfast. After eating all my flower bulbs, they shouldn't be too hungry. Before I sat down, I was already thinking of what to tell you about our Flag Day plans. Ethel and Henry have gotten me to agree to participate in the annual parade.
>
> Love,
> Ruth

Assignment

Answer Ruth's letter. Mrs. Quigley will want to tell her sister what happened on Flag Day in Lake Wobegon and how she felt about it. She will also probably comment on her health and the weather. Try to use the language and structures from the unit in your letter.

Garrison Keillor has this advice for how to get started on a personal letter:

Sit for a few minutes with a blank sheet in front of you, and meditate on the person you will write to. Let your friend come to mind until you can almost see her or him in the room with you. Remember the last time you saw each other and how your friend looked and what you said and what perhaps was unsaid between you, and when your friend becomes real to you, start to write.

UNIT 2

A Day at the Circus with Mazumbo

1 Judging from Experience

Read the questions. Discuss the answers with your classmates.

1. Look at the drawing. Why might the man be worried?
2. Look at the title. What do you think this story might be about?
3. Did you ever go to the circus as a child? What do you remember?

2 Listening

Part One

A Vocabulary

1 Complete the sentences with a word or expression from the box. Then compare your answers with those of a classmate. If you disagree, consult another classmate, a dictionary or your teacher. You will hear the italicized words in the story.

1. A *one-ring* circus can present only *one act at a time*.

2. The *trunk* of an elephant is its _____.

3. When a man does not shave for several days, his face becomes *bristly*. It is

   _____.

4. Riding in a boat or a plane makes some people feel *queasy*. They become

   _____.

5. At the supermarket, you can find fresh food and dried food; you can also find

   canned goods, which is food _____.

6. The *grocery store,* or _____, is where you buy food

   and household items.

7. The nickname for a small car produced by the Volkswagen company is

   _____.

8. Food supplies can also be called _____.

a) nose
b) hairy and rough
c) one act at a time
d) in cans
e) sick to their stomachs
f) *VW*
g) supermarket
h) *provisions*

2 Read the sentences and find the word or expression in the box that means the same as the italicized words. Then compare your answers with those of a classmate. If you disagree, consult another classmate, a dictionary or your teacher.

1. _____ The party was wonderful. There was food, music and dancing. Everybody was *whooping it up*.

2. _____ After packing all of our suitcases into the car, we *pulled out* of the driveway to begin the trip.

3. _____ The circus elephant was *staked* out in the field to keep her from walking away.

4. _____ I don't know how I'll find the time to finish all this work. I have a lot of *stuff* to do.

5. _____ At first, I couldn't find change for the bus, but then I *fished down* in my other pocket and found enough money.

6. _____ If you spend all the money in your wallet, you will *be out of* money.

7. _____ My father, who is tall, *banged* his head going through the low doorway.

> **a)** drove out
> **b)** reached deep inside
> **c)** activities
> **d)** becoming very noisy and excited
> **e)** tied to a metal or wooden stick in the ground
> **f)** not have any
> **g)** hit

B *Getting the Gist of the Story*

This is a story about Ed Buehler and his six children and their meeting with a circus elephant named Mazumbo, which they met when the Nobles and Norman Circus came to Lake Wobegon.

Listen to Part One of the story. Read the question and write your answer. Then compare your answer with those of your classmates.

What did the Buehlers do when they were out of peanuts?

_____

_____

_____

C Listening for Detail 🔊

Listen again to Part One. Decide whether each statement is true or false. Write *T* or *F* in the blank. Then compare your answers with those of a classmate. Listen again if you disagree with each other.

1. This circus travels around the countryside. __T__

2. The Buehlers' family car was a Volkswagen. _____

3. When the Buehler kids saw the elephant Mazumbo, she was walking around freely in the field. _____

4. Mazumbo was too old to participate in the circus anymore. _____

5. The Buehlers had bought a lot of peanuts at the circus. _____

6. Ed Buehler did not drive up too close to Mazumbo. _____

7. Ed was afraid because there was a snake in the car. _____

8. Mazumbo ate up all of the Buehlers' peanuts. _____

9. The children did not enjoy feeding the elephant. _____

10. Mazumbo put her two front feet up on the car. _____

Part Two

D Vocabulary

Circle the letter of the expression that is closest in meaning to the italicized word or phrase. Then compare your answers with those of a classmate.

1. Because the elephant was so large and so hungry, Ed was worried that she might become angry and *crush* the car.

   a) pull   **b)** scratch   **c)** flatten

2. Ed imagined the car as flat as a *pancake*.

   a) thin, soft cake   **b)** cake pan   **c)** table

3. He imagined that they might have an accident; then there would be a police *investigation* to discover the cause.

   a) search   **b)** chase   **c)** report

4. Newspaper stories often *reveal* interesting facts about politicians' personal lives.

    a) lie about   **b)** list   **c)** uncover

5. Ed's fears about the elephant grew until he *panicked*.

    a) lost his fear   **b)** lost control of himself   **c)** lost his balance

6. While he was in the car, Ed wondered if he should *back up*.

    a) get out and push the car   **b)** make the car go backwards

    c) get into the back of the car

7. Which line has *ridges*, like a mountain range?

    a)   **b)**   **c)**

8. The children were *tickling each other* and playing games.

    a) talking to each other   **b)** singing with each other

    c) touching each other to make each other laugh

9. An audience usually *quiets down* as soon as the orchestra begins to play.

    a) becomes sleepy   **b)** becomes happy   **c)** becomes less noisy

10. Children often say they will keep their rooms clean, but it is difficult for them to *keep a promise*.

    a) make a decision   **b)** do what they say they will do   **c)** find the time

E | Predicting and Listening

1 Working in small groups, discuss the question. Predict what might happen next in the story. Write down at least two possible answers.

How will Ed Buehler get his children away from the elephant?

    a. _____

    b. _____

2 Keeping your same groups, listen to the end of the story. Discuss how your predictions were different from the ending you heard.

F Listening for Detail

Listen again to Part Two. Decide whether each statement is true or false. Write *T* or *F* in the blank. Then compare your answers with those of a classmate. Listen again if you disagree with each other.

1. Ed's car was badly damaged by Mazumbo. _____

2. As they drove home, Ed was frightened but the children were not. _____

3. The Buehler children pretended that their arms were snakes. _____

4. Ed's feelings were so strong that he began to cry. _____

5. Ed did not drive home by the shortest route. Instead, he took more time than usual. _____

6. The children did not tell their mother anything about Mazumbo. _____

3 Getting the Joke

Read each item and decide which answer explains why the audience laughs. Circle your choice. Then, working in groups, compare your answers. If you agree, discuss the reasons for your choices. If you disagree, discuss your opinions and try to come to an agreement. In each case, there is one choice that best explains the joke.

1. "When they got done with the circus and they went outside, Ed and the six little kids, and they all got into the old VW, it was like a clown car."
The Buehler car is similar to a clown car because both are

   a) painted brightly.

   b) commonly seen at the circus.

   c) packed with people.

2. "By the time they got to the sixth handful of peanuts, Mazumbo had quite a bit of her trunk inside the car, feeling around in there and looking around for provisions, which kind of made Ed feel a little queasy because he's always had a fear of snakes."
Mazumbo's trunk reminded Ed of a snake because both are

   a) gray.

   b) long and thin.

   c) frightening.

3. "And then Mazumbo just kind of lifted her head a little bit. The left side of the VW went up about two feet. Oh, he could see it then: 'Family of Seven Crushed by Elephant. Car Flattened Like a Pancake. Investigation Reveals Father Error.' " Ed felt so guilty about endangering his children that he believed for a moment that

a) the circus officials would call the police.

b) he would have to kill the elephant.

c) his mistake would be announced in the headlines of the town newspaper.

4. Ed imagined that his car would be "flattened like a pancake" because the car

a) was not working properly.

b) was so old.

c) seemed so small.

 # 4 *Reviewing Vocabulary*

Fill in each blank with one of these words or expressions. Be sure to use the correct form of the italicized words. Compare your answers with those of a classmate.

whoop it up	*be* out of	*stake*	*fish* down
feel queasy	*tickle*	canned goods	*pull* out
keep *a* promise	crush	quiet down	

After the Nobles and Norman Circus, the Buehler children saw Mazumbo _____
₁

out in the field, and they begged their father to drive over to her. Each of the children fed her handfuls of

peanuts until they _____ peanuts. Then Mazumbo ate up all the other food: the
₂

Oreo cookies, candy bars and potato chips. Ed _____ in the grocery sack for more
₃

food to feed Mazumbo, but all he could find were _____.
₄

While the children _____ with the elephant, Ed began to _____
₅ ₆

because her trunk reminded him of a very large snake. He imagined that Mazumbo might

_____ the car and all of his children. Even after he _____
₇ ₈

of the parking lot, the children could not _____. They _____
₉ ₁₀

each other and pretended that their arms were elephant trunks. Although they had said they would not tell

their mother about the experience with Mazumbo, they were too excited to _____.
₁₁

5 | Interpreting the Characters

Read the following questions and answers. The answers are not mentioned directly in the story, but it is possible to make good guesses based on your knowledge of the story and of American life. Decide whether each answer is *likely* or *unlikely*. Circle your choice. Then, working in small groups, give reasons for your choices and discuss your opinions. There is no one correct answer, but there is more evidence for some choices than for others.

1. Why did Ed say yes when the children asked to feed Mazumbo?

  a) They had too many peanuts, and he wanted to get rid   *likely*   *unlikely*
  of them.

  b) He wanted to see the elephant up close, too.   *likely*   *unlikely*

  c) The children were so noisy that he wanted them to   *likely*   *unlikely*
  quiet down.

2. Why did Ed make the children promise not to tell their mother about Mazumbo?

  a) He felt that she would be angry with him.   *likely*   *unlikely*

  b) He did not want his wife to feel that she had missed   *likely*   *unlikely*
  all the fun.

  c) He thought that their mother probably would not be   *likely*   *unlikely*
  interested.

6 | Retelling the Story

Use these phrases to retell the story in your own words. As you speak, try to include as many details as you can. A different student may want to retell each part.

This information may help you:

The six Buehler children and their father went
to the circus one day . . .

- clown car
- elephant
- stay in the car
- feed
- peanuts

The children fed Mazumbo handfuls of
peanuts . . .

- trunk inside the car
- fear of snakes
- out of peanuts
- laughing
- banged his head
- more food

Mazumbo lifted her head and the left side of
the VW went up about two feet . . .

- newspaper headline
- Ed panicked
- backed up
- arms like trunks
- World's Greatest Dad
- sweat and tears running
  down his face
- promise
- told everything

7 | *Telling Your Own Stories*

1 Find out which classmates have had the following experiences. Ask yes/no
questions: for example, "Have you ever had a frightening experience with an
animal?" Try to find one classmate for each statement. When you get a "yes"
answer, write that classmate's name in the blank. Do not tell any stories yet. To
begin the exercise, stand up and move around the classroom freely.

1. _____ has had a frightening experience with an animal.
      (name)

2. _____ had felt like a bad parent.
      (name)

3. _____ has had to keep a secret.
      (name)

4. _____ has been written about in a newspaper.
      (name)

2 Look at your list above. If several of you have stories for each experience, one
of you should volunteer to be the storyteller. You can tell your stories to the
whole class or to small groups. If almost everyone has a story to tell, you
might want to work in pairs and exchange stories.

8 | Getting into the Language

A | Notice the Structure: Newspaper Headlines

> **Family of Seven Crushed by Elephant**
> **Car Flattened Like a Pancake**
> **Investigation Reveals Father Error**

Newspaper headlines are written in a special language. Read these general guidelines and examples.

- Auxiliary verbs (*is, was, were, has, have, had*), *be* (as the main verb), articles and some prepositions are omitted.

  A family was crushed by an elephant.
  Family Crushed by Elephant

- The present tense often refers to past action.

  An investigation has revealed an error by a father.
  Investigation Reveals Father Error

- The present participle often expresses present action.

  The police are investigating a father.
  Police Investigating Father

- Infinitives refer to future action.

  Children are going to donate gifts.
  Children to Donate Gifts

- Compound nouns are common.

  The workers are entering a fight over their contract.
  Workers to Enter Contract Fight

- The first word and all other words, except for prepositions and articles, are capitalized.

  A circus will appear at the ballpark.
  Circus to Appear at Ballpark

B | Practice the Structure

1 Here are some headlines that might appear above newspaper stories. Add the missing words.

a. Prof. Kratz to Speak Monday at L.W. High

Professor Katz is going to speak on Monday at Lake Wobegon High School.

b. Two Injured in Weekend Car Accident

_____

c. John Ewing Wins 800 Meter at L.W. High

_____

d. City Investigating Hospital Construction Delays

_____

e. Hospital Chairman Bunsen to Address City Council Tuesday

_____

f. Minneapolis Museum Buys Van Gogh for $3.5 M

_____

2 Create a headline from the first sentence of the news or sports story below.
You will not always use all of the words from the sentence in the headline.

a. Headline: _St. Cloud Council to study School Recreation Plan_

The Saint Cloud City Council is going to study the recreation plan of the school district.

b. Headline: _____

A number of new rules at the hospital have raised medical costs.

c. Headline: _____

The New York Yankees won against the Minnesota Twins in the opening game of the World Series.

d. Headline: _____

The state government is studying a plan for a new subway in the capital city.

e. Headline: _____

Twenty people were trapped in a highrise elevator.

f. Headline: _____

A damaged airplane landed safely at the municipal airport last night in heavy fog.

_____

3 Write two headlines about recent news or sports events in your country.

a. _____

b. _____

4 Read a local newspaper in English. Add the missing words to the headlines.

9 Extending the Story in Writing

A Writing Down a Story

Write down a story from Exercise 7, either one you heard or your own. If you choose another student's story, show your work to the storyteller when you finish. Ask the storyteller to comment on your version. Then revise the story, making any necessary changes and corrections.

B Writing a Feature Article

A newspaper includes several kinds of articles. Feature stories, unlike straight news stories, are meant to entertain as well as to inform. They are longer than news articles because the writer takes time to describe people, give examples and create a mood. Often, features use special devices such as odd facts or questions to attract a reader's attention.

Model

Notice the organization and style of this excerpt from a feature on Flag Day in an old issue of the Lake Wobegon newspaper.

Lake Wobegon Herald-Star

June 15, 1936　　　　　**Lake Wobegon, Minnesota**　　**5¢**

**Farm Bureau Concurs:
Farmers Should Not Pay**

The president of the Minnesota Farm Bureau opposes taxing the farmers to establish a fund to cover bankruptcies of milk buyers.

Various plans have surfaced since about 100 farmers, some in our county, were unpaid for 30 to 45 days of milk production by the Marker Company in St. Cloud, which filed for bankruptcy.

Last week Stangel argued that it was not the farmers' responsibility to obtain the money. He said, "the burden of establishing any fund should be put upon the purchasers, the manufacturers."

Citizens Form Flag
Unique Flag Day Celebration

What has over 800 legs and is red, white and blue? If you had been on Main Street last week, you would know the answer. Hjalmar Ingqvist organized a sight never seen here before.

It seems that people were looking for a new way to participate in a Flag Day celebration. The idea of creating a human flag with red, white and blue caps appealed to a lot of citizens.

"It was beautiful," remarked Mrs. Quigley, one of the many Lake Wobegonians who participated in the living flag. "We all felt moved to be part of something so lovely to honor our country."

This sentiment was echoed by many, although nobody failed to mention the intense heat.

Assignment

For next week's edition of the *Lake Wobegon Herald-Star,* write a feature article about the Buehlers' unusual experience with Mazumbo the elephant. As the reporter, you have interviewed the whole family, but you have decided to write from the children's point of view. Be sure to write a headline for your piece.

UNIT 3
Bruno, the Fishing Dog

1 Judging from Experience

Read the questions. Discuss the answers with your classmates.

Look at the drawing. What is this dog trying to do? Do you think that he will be successful?

2 Listening

Part One

A Vocabulary

Read the sentences and find the word or expression in the box that means the same as the italicized words. Then compare your answers with those of a classmate. If you disagree, consult another classmate, a dictionary or your teacher.

1. _____ In a small town, reading the *social notes column* of the newspaper is a way to find out what is happening to everybody in town.

2. _____ If a person does not want to go into the deep water, he or she can simply *wade around* at the edge.

3. _____ Many water plants and animals live in the *shallows* at the edge of a lake.

4. _____ People put *bait* on the end of a fishing line to catch fish.

5. _____ When people go fishing in Minnesota lakes, they hope to be able to catch a *walleye*.

6. _____ The kitten *batted* its toy around the room.

7. _____ Dogs can chew bones because they have very powerful *jaws*.

8. _____ If someone catches a prize fish, everyone *makes a fuss over* it.

a) walk in water

b) food used to attract fish, animals or birds

c) the section that lists personal and family news such as births, marriages, visits or parties

d) pays a lot of attention to

e) areas that are not deep

f) a fish famous for its ability to get itself loose from a fish hook

g) hit playfully

h) bones and muscles of the mouth

B Getting the Gist of the Story 📼

This is a story about a woman, Lena Johnson, and an old friend, Bruno. Bruno is a dog that belongs to Lena's son, Bob.

Listen to Part One of the story. Read the question and write your answer. Then compare your answer with those of your classmates.

How did Bruno become known as a "fishing dog"?

_____

C Listening for Detail 📼

Listen again to Part One. Decide whether each statement is true or false. Write *T* or *F* in the blank. Then compare your answers with those of a classmate. Listen again if you disagree with each other.

1. Bruno's name was in the newspaper. _____

2. Bruno lives in Minneapolis with Mrs. Lena Johnson. _____

3. Lena's son, Bob, and his wife, Merlette, enjoy spending a lot of time with

Lena. _____

4. Bruno is about 14 years old. _____

Part Two

D Vocabulary

1 Read the sentences and find the word or expression in the box that means the same as the italicized words. Then compare your answers with those of a classmate. If you disagree, consult another classmate, a dictionary or your teacher.

1. _____ People often put their address on a pet's *collar* so the animal can be returned if it gets lost.

2. _____ It is possible to move a heavy object by getting in front of it and *towing* it.

3. _____ When pet owners walk with their dogs, they often use a *leash* to control the animal's movement.

4. _____ If a dog sees another dog or a cat, it might suddenly *bolt* from its owner.

5. _____ In the summertime, many homes use a *screen door* to let air in but keep insects out of the house.

6. _____ Children like to eat *Jell-O* because it shakes in a funny way on the plate.

7. _____ A popular kind of citrus fruit is the *mandarin orange.*

8. _____ *Marshmallows* are delicious when they are cooked over a fire or put in different desserts.

9. _____ Potato chips or raw vegetables are often served with some sort of *cream dip.*

10. _____ *Trout* is very tasty when it is fried or smoked.

11. _____ People often wear an *apron* when they cook.

a) run away

b) pulling

c) a soft food often made with sour cream or cream cheese and various spices

d) special door that is made of fine wire net

e) cloth worn over the front of one's clothes to keep them clean

f) a small fruit that easily breaks into separate pieces

g) a long piece of chain, cloth or leather used to hold an animal

h) short piece of chain, cloth or leather tied around an animal's neck

i) a kind of very soft, white candy

j) a popular type of fish

k) fruit-flavored gelatin dessert

2 Circle the letter of the expression that is closest in meaning to the italicized word or phrase. Then compare your answers with those of a classmate.

1. The children were so excited that when they got out of the car, they went *straight* to the water.

   a) slowly   **b)** carefully   **c)** directly

2. Sometimes when we need our family the most, our own *flesh and blood* can disappoint us.

   a) relative   **b)** body   **c)** best friend

3. After many ceremonial occasions, such as a baptism or a wedding, there is *a reception* for the guests.

   a) a gift   **b)** a party   **c)** an announcement

4. Instead of serving a formal meal to a large group, people may choose to have a *buffet*.

   a) a sandwich   **b)** an outdoor meal   **c)** a serve-yourself meal

5. People often use *caterers* when they do not have time to prepare beautiful party meals at home themselves.

   a) fast food   **b)** professional cooks   **c)** frozen dinners

6. When you are giving a large party, it is important to have everything *under control* before the guests arrive.

   a) in order   **b)** on the table   **c)** written down

E Getting the Gist of the Story

Listen to Part Two of the story. Read the question and write your answer. Then compare your answer with those of your classmates.

How did Lena Johnson feel at the home of her son, Bob, and his wife, Merlette?

_____

F Listening for Detail

Listen again to Part Two. Decide whether each statement is true or false. Write *T* or *F* in the blank. Then compare your answers with those of a classmate. Listen again if you disagree with each other.

1. Bruno spent most of July and August fishing in Lake Wobegon. _____

2. Bruno did not catch any fish at Lake Wobegon this year. _____

3. Lena went to visit her son for the baptism of her grandchild. _____

4. Bruno was rather old and might not have lived long enough to come back to Lake Wobegon the next summer. _____

5. Bruno obeyed Lena very well. _____

6. Lena was pleased to see all the guests at her son's house. _____

7. When she arrived at her son's house, Lena went directly to the kitchen to help. _____

8. The caterers were very happy that Lena had brought a Jello salad. _____

9. There was a turkey in the middle of the buffet table. _____

10. Lena saw Bruno standing outside the screen door. _____

Part Three

G Vocabulary

Read the sentences and find the word or expression in the box that means the same as the italicized words. Then compare your answers with those of a classmate. If you disagree, consult another classmate, a dictionary or your teacher.

1. _____ A hunting dog will *freeze* when it smells a rabbit.

2. _____ A dog's *hind* legs bend the opposite way from its front legs.

3. _____ The ballet dancer crossed the stage in only a few *leaps*.

4. _____ Some people put a rubber or plastic *pad* under the tablecloth to protect the table.

5. _____ If you try to stop a car too quickly when there is ice, snow or rain on the road, the car may *skid*.

6. _____ It often takes weeks to clean up the *wreckage* from a plane crash.

7. _____ If you drop a book on a hard floor, it sounds like a *slap*.

8. _____ When you set the table for a buffet, put the *silverware* next to the plates and napkins.

9. _____ After a party, some people like to *straighten* everything *out* right away, but others wait until later.

10. _____ After a party, there is usually a *mess* in the kitchen.

11. _____ Sometimes two rooms are connected by an *arch*.

12. _____ One job of a host or hostess is to ask what kind of drinks the guests *care for*.

a) jumps
b) broken parts
c) knives, forks and spoons
d) doorway with a rounded top
e) quick hit with the flat part of the hand
f) slip sideways
g) back
h) state of disorder
i) stop suddenly
j) soft cover
k) clean up
l) want

H Predicting and Listening

1 Working in small groups, discuss the question. Predict what might happen next in the story. Write down at least two possible answers.

What will Bruno do if Lena lets him into the house during the reception?

a. _____

b. _____

c. _____

2 Keeping your same groups, listen to the end of the story. Discuss how your predictions were different from the ending you heard.

I Listening for Detail

Listen again to Part Three. Circle the letter of the answer that best completes each sentence. Then compare your answers with those of a classmate. Listen again if you disagree with each other.

1. When Lena opened the screen door, Bruno _____ into the house.

a) looked

b) walked

c) bolted

2. Bruno leaped onto the table in order to

a) get the fish.

b) slide along it.

c) pull off the tablecloth.

3. After he got what he wanted, Bruno

a) calmed down.

b) escaped through the screen door.

c) went into the kitchen.

4. Bruno knocked the entire buffet onto the floor, so _____ cleaned up the wreckage.

a) Bob and Merlette

b) the caterers

c) Lena

5. After the mess was all cleaned up, Lena offered the guests some

a) coffee.

b) Jell-O.

c) clean plates.

3 Getting the Joke

Read each item and decide which answer explains why the audience laughs. Circle your choice. Then, working in groups, compare your answers. If you agree, discuss the reasons for your choices. If you disagree, discuss your opinions and try to come to an agreement. In each case, there is one choice that best explains the joke.

1. "That's, I guess, why he was visiting in Lake Wobegon July and August: in order to do some fishing down at the lake." Visitors that go to a lake for summer vacation are usually

a) patient.

b) human.

c) happy.

2. "That dog caught a six-pound walleye." Catching a walleye is _____ for a dog than it is for a human.

a) more important

b) easier

c) more difficult

3. "She was going to put on an apron and help, but there at the sink were two women in white dresses, identical white dresses . . . . They were caterers!" Lena thought that using caterers at a party in one's own home was

a) expensive.

b) unnecessary.

c) a good idea.

4. "She looked up and saw that Bruno's eyes were locked onto that smoked trout." Lena was worried because she knew that Bruno had

a) fishing experience.

b) a big appetite.

c) good eyesight.

5. "Then she was there, under the arch. Lena was there, holding out a plate of cherry Jell-O with mandarin oranges. She said, 'Would anybody care for dessert?'" Just like Bruno, Lena had proved that she was

a) hungry.

b) old.

c) talented.

4 Reviewing Vocabulary

Fill in each blank with one of these words or expressions. Be sure to use the correct form of the italicized words. Compare your answers with those of a classmate.

skid	care for	*bolt*	reception
wade	flesh and blood	*freeze*	straighten things out
caterer	leap	straight	under control

make a fuss over

When Bruno, Bob and Merlette Johnson's dog, was about a year old, he caught a fish while he

_____ around in the shallows in Lake Wobegon. He hit it with his paw a few

1

times, then grabbed it in his mouth. It was a six-pound walleye! Everyone in the town

_____ Bruno and his fish.

2

Bruno spent all of his summers with Lena Johnson, Bob's mother. Although he went

_____ down to the lake to look for fish as soon as he arrived every summer,

3

Bruno did not have much luck catching another fish. This year, Bruno was about 14 years old. When Lena

drove him back home to Minneapolis, it was as if he had missed his last chance.

Lena brought Bruno back home to Bob and Merlette's house on the day of a formal

_____ to celebrate the baptism of their youngest child. Although Bob and his child

4

are Lena's own _____, their way of life made her feel uncomfortable. She felt like

5

a stranger in their home.

Bob and Merlette had hired _____ to prepare a very fancy buffet dinner. The

6

table was covered with food, including a large smoked trout in the middle. Lena let her friend Bruno into

the house, and when he saw the enormous fish on the table, he _____. Then,

7

suddenly, he _____ over to the table, made a long _____

8   9

up onto it and grabbed the fish. Because there was no pad under the tablecloth, he

_____ down the entire length of the table, knocking everything onto the floor. As

10

Bruno escaped out the back door, Lena calmly tried to _____. When she got

11

everything _____, she proudly asked the guests if they would

_____ some of her cherry Jell-O with mandarin oranges and tiny marshmallows for

dessert.

5 Interpreting the Characters

Read the following questions and answers. The answers are not mentioned directly in the story, but it is possible to make good guesses based on your knowledge of the story and of American life. Decide whether each answer is *likely* or *unlikely*. Circle your choice. Then, working in small groups, give reasons for your choices and discuss your opinions. There is no one correct answer, but there is more evidence for some choices than for others.

1. Bob and Merlette Johnson have been bringing their dog, Bruno, up to Lake Wobegon every summer to stay with Lena. Why did they leave Bruno there all summer if they themselves visited for only one day this year?

   a) They wanted to make sure that Lena had some company, someone for her to talk to.　　　　*likely*　　*unlikely*

   b) They wanted to give Bruno one last summer of fishing in the country because he was so old.　　　　*likely*　　*unlikely*

   c) They were tired of the dog's bad behavior and wanted to get him out of their house.　　　　*likely*　　*unlikely*

2. When Lena offered her cherry Jell-O with mandarin oranges and tiny marshmallows to the caterers at her son's house, they put it in the refrigerator and said that Merlette Johnson, Lena's daughter-in-law, would use it later in the week. Why did the caterers not want to use the Jell-O?

   a) They already had enough food.　　　　*likely*　　*unlikely*

   b) They wanted to save Lena's gift for Bob and Merlette to enjoy alone later.　　　　*likely*　　*unlikely*

   c) They did not think it looked as nice as the food they had prepared.　　　　*likely*　　*unlikely*

6 | Retelling the Story

Use these phrases to retell the story in your own words. As you speak, try to
include as many details as you can. A different student may want to retell each
part.

This information may help you:

There was an item in the newspaper . . .
- social notes column
- Bruno
- Lena Johnson
- Bob and Merlette
- for only one day

Bruno is a fishing dog . . .
- a year old
- wade around
- shallows
- six-pound walleye
- make a fuss
- all July and August
- never caught another fish
- 14 years old

Lena took Bruno back to the Cities . . .
- baptism
- own flesh and blood
- reception
- Jell-O
- caterers
- screen door
- smoked trout
- wreckage
- under the arch
- dessert

7 | Telling Your Own Stories

1 Find out which classmates have had the following experiences. Ask yes/no
questions: for example, "Have you ever owned a pet that did something unusual
or had a special talent?" Try to find one classmate for each statement. When
you get a "yes" answer, write that classmate's name in the blank. Do not tell
any stories yet. To begin the exercise, stand up and move around the classroom
freely.

1. _____ has owned a pet that did something unusual or had a
   (name)   special talent.

2. _____ has felt that he or she did not really know a family
   (name)   member very well.

3. _____ spent a childhood summer in a special place.
   (name)

4. _____ has given a gift that was not appreciated.
   (name)

2 Look at your list above. If several of you have stories for each experience, one
of you should volunteer to be the storyteller. You can tell your stories to the
whole class or to small groups. If almost everyone has a story to tell, you
might want to work in pairs and exchange stories.

8 Getting into the Language

A Notice the Structure: would

> The dog **would go** straight down to the lake.

There are many different uses for the verb *would*. Sometimes we use *would* + VERB to talk about past habits. It is just like *used to* + VERB. Another use of *would* is to talk about the future from the point of view of a past time. This is called "the future in the past." It is like *was going to* + VERB. Compare these two uses of *would* in the sentence below.

> When Bruno visited Lake Wobegon, he **would** always **go** straight down to the lake because he thought that he **would catch** another fish.

The first example of *would* refers to a repeated past action; Bruno had a habit of going down to the lake. The second example of *would* refers to something that Bruno thought was going to happen.

B Practice the Structure

Read the following passage. Notice the underlined words. Some of them refer to past habits, and some of them refer to expectations about the future from a past perspective. In the blanks on the right, write either *P-H* (for "past habit") or *F-P* (for "future in the past") for each verb.

Every summer for the past fourteen years, Bob Johnson <u>would bring</u> his dog,
₁

Bruno, up to Lake Wobegon to spend the summer with Bob's mother, Lena. The

two of them <u>would spend</u> many hours down at the lake. Bruno
₂

<u>would stand and stare</u> at the water endlessly, hoping that he <u>would see</u> another
₃   ₄

walleye like the one he had caught when he was a young dog.

Since he <u>would wade around</u> in the shallows so often, there was a good chance
₅

that he <u>would get</u> a fish at least once. Last summer he almost caught another large
₆

fish. He saw it and tried to grab it in his jaws, but he did not act quickly enough,

so the fish got away. That missed opportunity, however, gave Bruno a renewed

interest in life and fishing, and he spent the rest of the season in the same part of

the lake, expecting that the same fish <u>would return</u>.
₇

1. _P-H_

2. _____

3. _____

4. _____

5. _____

6. _____

7. _____

9 Extending the Story in Writing

A Writing Down a Story

Write down a story from Exercise 7, either one you heard or your own. If you choose another student's story, show your work to the storyteller when you finish. Ask the storyteller to comment on your version. Then revise the story, making any necessary changes and corrections.

B Giving Directions

When you invite someone to your home for the first time, it is important to give the person clear directions for getting there. There are several words and expressions that are commonly used to help people find places they have never been to before.

Look at the following information.

prepositions

from the north, the south, the east, the west (To indicate the direction that one is traveling from)
on the left, right **or** *on* your left, right (To indicate something located on the side)
at the second light (To indicate the position of something at a particular point)

verbs

take Route 138 (To indicate the correct road to travel on)
take the second left (To indicate where and how to turn)
make a right (To indicate where and how to turn)
head south (To indicate the correct direction of travel)
keep on going downtown (To indicate the correct way to continue)
when you *hit* Main Street (To indicate encountering something: a road, a town, etc.)
get off at the Pearl St. exit (To indicate where to leave a highway)

nouns

blocks (The divisions of a city by streets into small sections; the distance from one street to the next)
fork (A place where a road divides into two separate directions)
exit (The place where one gets off a highway)
landmark (A building, a tree, a rock or something that the traveler will easily recognize, and that will help him or her find the way)

adjectives

southbound, northbound, etc. (Going in the direction of south, north, etc.)
a *hard* right turn **or** a *sharp* left turn (A turn at a corner where the two roads meet at an acute angle, less than 90°)
an *immediate* left (A turn that is made just after another turn or a particular landmark)

Model

Read the following directions for getting to the church where Bob and Merlette Johnson had the baptism for their child. These driving directions were sent to their friends and relatives from out of town.

Directions to the Church for the Johnson Baptism

From the north take Route 35 southbound. When the road forks north of town, take the right fork, route 35W.

Get off of route 35W at the West Lake Street exit. Head west on West Lake Street for about one mile.

Make a left onto Hennepin Avenue, and keep on going down Hennepin to West 36th Street. When you hit West 36th Street, take a right.

Then, a landmark for you will be the big pine tree on your left. There, you take an immediate, hard left into the church parking lot.

(If you continue on down past the church, you'll pass Lake Harriet and Lyndale Park. If you see the Minnesota Transportation Museum, you'll know you've gone too far.)

Assignment

When Bob and Merlette had the baptism for their youngest child, they held a reception at their house after the ceremony. Many of the people who came had never been to their house before, so they needed directions for how to get from the church to the house. Look at the map below and write the directions as clearly as you can.

From the church, turn left onto West 36th Street . . .

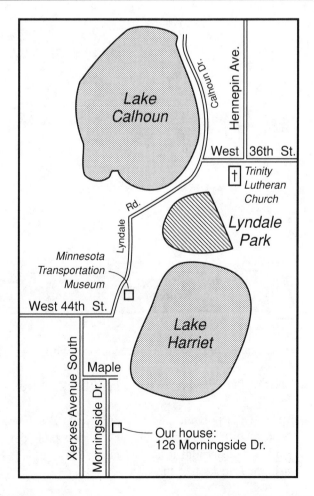

UNIT 4
Sylvester Krueger's Desk

1 Judging from Experience

Read the questions. Discuss the answers with your classmates.

1. Look at the drawing. What might the boy be looking at on the underside of his desk?
2. Look at the portraits of U.S. presidents Washington and Lincoln. Judging from these pictures, how would you describe their personalities?
3. This is a classroom in an old elementary school. Have you ever seen old-fashioned desks like these?

Part One

A Vocabulary

1 Read the sentences and find the word or expression in the box that means the same as the italicized words. Then compare your answers with those of a classmate. If you disagree, consult another classmate, a dictionary or your teacher.

1. _____ In the U.S., *Labor Day* is always celebrated on the first Monday in September.

2. _____ Some people believe that *Adam* was the first man on Earth.

3. _____ *Floor wax* can make even old floors look new again.

4. _____ A new *coat* of paint can make a room look brighter and bigger.

5. _____ It is common for public buildings to have *portraits* on the walls.

6. _____ A person who is *prim* rarely enjoys jokes.

7. _____ Many schools offer classes in *dental hygiene* as part of the students' health education.

8. _____ Rather than buying new things for their homes, some people like to collect *antiques*.

9. _____ *Ancient,* as well as modern, coins have the faces of heroes on them.

10. _____ Sometimes there are *lumps* of old chewing gum under school desks.

11. _____ Very often, *janitors* work at night, after most people have gone home.

12. _____ Sometimes lovers *carve* their names into the trunk of a tree.

a) layer

b) easily shocked by anything improper

c) a holiday to honor working men and women

d) paintings, drawings or photographs of real people

e) cut

f) pieces of furniture, jewelry, etc., that are old and valuable

g) the husband of Eve

h) polish for floors

i) masses of something solid with no special size or shape

j) very old

k) people who clean offices or buildings

l) care of the teeth

2 Circle the letter of the expression that is closest in meaning to the italicized word or phrase. Then compare your answers with those of a classmate.

1. Most of the questions on the exam were easy, but there was one question that the student did not understand. He was *stumped*.

   a) tired   **b)** cheated   **c)** unable to answer

2. Children can be very cruel. They often *make fun of* each other's hair and other physical features.

   a) laugh at   **b)** draw   **c)** try to copy

3. Some people's hair becomes very *frizzy* when they go out in the rain.

   a) wet   **b)** curly   **c)** dark

4. In some schools in the countryside, children of many different ages *are apt to* study together because there are not enough teachers.

   a) know how to   **b)** prefer to   **c)** are likely to

5. Sometimes it is a good idea to *hold on to* old clothing and furniture rather than throw it away, because it can be used again later.

   a) keep   **b)** remember   **c)** give away

6. Over millions of years, trees and other living things can *become petrified*.

   a) be forgotten   **b)** get lost   **c)** turn into rock

B Getting the Gist of the Story

This is a story about Garrison when he was in elementary school in 1951. It is September, the beginning of the school year in Lake Wobegon.

Listen to Part One of the story. Read the question and write your answer. Then compare your answer with those of your classmates.

What did Garrison find carved into his desk at school?

_____

C Listening for Detail

Listen again to Part One. Decide whether each statement is true or false. Write *T* or *F* in the blank. Then compare your answers with those of a classmate. Listen again if you disagree with each other.

1. The school year has always started on a Monday in Lake Wobegon. _____

2. When the children came back to school, few things had changed. _____

3. The portraits of Lincoln and Washington were on the classroom wall. _____

4. Garrison liked Lincoln more than he liked Washington. _____

5. Garrison sometimes gave answers to other students. _____

6. George Washington had bad teeth. _____

7. The oldest carving on Garrison's desk was more than fifty years old. _____

Part Two

D Vocabulary

Read the sentences and find the word or expression in the box that means the same as the italicized words. Then compare your answers with those of a classmate. If you disagree, consult another classmate, a dictionary or your teacher.

1. _____ A public building or memorial often has a *brass plaque,* which gives important information, such as names or dates or famous sayings.

2. _____ "*In memoriam*" is often written on a war monument.

3. _____ School children often chew on paper and make *gobs* to throw at each other.

4. _____ A child often tries to *live up to* his or her parents' expectations and desires.

5. _____ A child who does not do well on an exam in school may feel that he has *let* his parents *down.*

6. _____ A *doorknob* can be made of wood, metal or glass.

7. _____ People who are very successful often become too *stuck-up* to talk with their old friends.

8. _____ When parents talk to their friends, they often *brag about* their children's achievements.

9. _____ A teacher usually has a *classroom monitor* to help with everyday activities.

10. _____ Sometimes children get too excited and *yank* toys from each other.

a) masses of something wet and sticky

b) disappointed

c) pull suddenly

d) proud

e) speak proudly of

f) in memory of

g) round object that one pulls to open a door

h) metal plate with writing on it

i) student who acts as an assistant

j) be able to meet the standards of living and behavior set by others

E Getting the Gist of the Story

Listen to Part Two of the story. Read the question and write your answer. Then compare your answer with those of your classmates.

Garrison was always worried that his teacher, Mrs. Meyers, might do something. What was it?

_____

F Listening for Detail

Listen again to Part Two. Circle the letter of the answer that best completes each sentence. Then compare your answers with those of a classmate. Listen again if you disagree with each other.

1. Garrison found the name *Sylvester Krueger* carved into the top of his desk. He also saw it

   a) in a library book.

   b) on the door.

   c) on a plaque.

2. Sylvester Krueger probably went to France as a

   a) soldier.

   b) tourist.

   c) student.

3. When Garrison realized that he was sitting at Sylvester's desk, he felt

   a) curious.

   b) proud.

   c) scared.

4. Garrison's teacher, Mrs. Meyers, said that she _____ Sylvester.

   a) did not know

   b) did not like

   c) remembered

5. Mrs. Meyers wanted Garrison to _____ Sylvester.

   a) forget about

   b) act like

   c) talk about

6. Mrs. Meyers thought that Garrison was the one who played a trick on Darla Ingqvist by putting a gob on the doorknob because he

   a) laughed so loudly.

   b) was close to the door.

   c) loved Darla.

7. Darla Ingqvist liked to _____ her money.

   a) spend

   b) share

   c) brag about

Part Three

G Vocabulary

Read the sentences and find the word or expression in the box that means the same as the italicized words. Then compare your answers with those of a classmate. If you disagree, consult another classmate, a dictionary or your teacher.

1. _____ A public building often has a *cloakroom*, where people can leave their belongings.

2. _____ The celebration of *Arbor Day* is important in the Midwestern part of the U.S. because so much of the area is grassland.

3. _____ *The Gettysburg Address*, delivered in 1863, became an important inspiration for the North during the U.S. Civil War.

4. _____ When you plant a tree, it is important to *tap* the earth around the trunk.

5. _____ Sometimes even a small *sliver* of a tree can grow into a big tree.

6. _____ In most places in the U.S., school *is out* for summer vacation by the second week in June.

7. _____ You play baseball or softball on a *diamond*.

8. _____ While playing sports, sometimes one person *stomps* on another person's foot.

9. _____ If a baseball player hits a *double or a triple*, the people watching the game usually cheer loudly.

10. _____ Sometimes people who are walking or running do not see rocks on the ground and *trip*.

a) small, thin, pointed piece of wood

b) steps on hard

c) room where coats, hats and umbrellas are kept

d) catch their foot and lose their balance

e) a speech made by Abraham Lincoln

f) press lightly on

g) playing field

h) is finished

i) a play in baseball in which the player hits the ball so far that he or she has time to run to two or three out of the four bases

j) an American holiday on which people plant trees

H | Predicting and Listening 📼

1 Working in small groups, discuss the question. Predict what might happen next in the story. Write down at least two possible answers.

Someone in Garrison's class tried to become a hero to the other children by playing a trick on Darla Ingqvist. Besides doing that, what are some of the ways that a schoolboy like Garrison could become a hero in the eyes of his classmates?

a. _____

b. _____

c. _____

2 Keeping your same groups, listen to the end of the story. Discuss how your predictions were different from the ending you heard.

I | Listening for Detail 📼

Listen again to Part Three. Decide whether each statement is true or false. Write T or F in the blank. Then compare your answers with those of a classmate. Listen again if you disagree with each other.

1. Garrison was punished for the trick that was played on Darla Ingqvist. _____

2. Mrs Meyers made Garrison change his seat for the rest of the year. _____

3. In the spring, the school held a ceremony in memory of the men who had died

in war. _____

4. Darla Ingqvist was chosen to plant the tree. _____

5. The tree was young and healthy. _____

6. The students gave the tree plenty of water. _____

7. The tree was planted in a well-chosen place. _____

8. Garrison hit a triple at the all-school picnic. _____

3 *Getting the Joke*

Read each item and decide which answer explains why the audience laughs. Circle your choice. Then, working in groups, compare your answers. If you agree, discuss the reasons for your choices. If you disagree, discuss your opinions and try to come to an agreement. In each case, there is one choice that best explains the joke.

1. "[Garrison] usually looked at Lincoln. He looked more sympathetic, like he might give an answer to a kid, you know. If you looked at him long enough, you might see his lips move. He'd say, 'Eight.' "
   Heroes like Abraham Lincoln do not usually

   a) talk.

   b) cheat.

   c) know math.

2. "Washington looked, I don't know, he looked like he had a headache or something."
   In their portraits, famous people do not usually seem to be

   a) serious.

   b) happy.

   c) in pain.

3. "I told Mrs. Meyers about it, which was a mistake . . . . Mrs. Meyers remembered what a good boy Sylvester Krueger always was, what a good student, and how he never made any trouble. Always was good. And she said, 'That gives you a lot to live up to, doesn't it?' "
   If Garrison had not mentioned Sylvester Krueger to Mrs. Meyers, she might not have

   a) compared Garrison to Sylvester.

   b) remembered Sylvester.

   c) noticed Garrison.

4. "Somebody put a big glob on the doorknob of the classroom, which Darla Ingqvist touched with her hand. But I didn't do it. Mrs. Meyers thought I did, because I was the one who laughed the loudest."
   People who play tricks on others usually

   a) are embarrassed.

   b) are impolite.

   c) keep quiet.

5. "Just a little sliver of a tree. Didn't even have any leaves on it, didn't look like it would last long, even though we watered it every day. And it didn't last long either."
   We usually think that memorials to the dead should be

   a) stone.

   b) permanent.

   c) metal.

4 Reviewing Vocabulary

Fill in each blank with one of these words or expressions. Be sure to use the correct form of the italicized words. Then compare your answers with those of a classmate.

let down	stumped	*make* fun of
portrait	*be* out	live up to
be apt to	*carve*	stuck-up
brag about	brass plaque	*hold* on to

When Garrison was a boy, he sat at his school desk and looked up at the _____ 1 of Lincoln and Washington on the classroom wall. When he was _____ 2 by a question the teacher asked, he looked at Lincoln because he thought that Lincoln seemed more sympathetic. He even imagined that Lincoln might _____ 3 give an answer to a child. Washington seemed disapproving, and Garrison thought that it might have been because people _____ 4 Washington's frizzy hair.

Since the town of Lake Wobegon did not have a lot of money, the school _____ 5 its old desks and other equipment for many years. On the old desk tops there were names and dates _____ 6 deeply into the wood. One of the most memorable ones for Garrison said, "SYLVESTER KRUEGER '31." This name also appeared on a _____ 7 in the school that listed the names of the students who had died in World War II. Garrison tried to _____ 8 the example set by his hero, Sylvester.

Sometimes Garrison felt that he _____ 9 his teacher and his hero. For example, once he almost had to move from Sylvester's desk when he laughed at a trick that was played on Darla Ingqvist, a _____ 10 little girl who always brought money to school and _____ 11 it.

In spite of that incident, the teacher let Garrison stay at his desk. And at the end of the school year, when school _____ almost _____ 12, he became a small hero himself when he hit a double at the all-school picnic softball game. Ironically, at this game, the tree planted in memory of the war dead was accidentally stomped on by a ball player.

5 | Interpreting the Characters

Read the following questions and answers. The answers are not mentioned directly
in the story, but it is possible to make good guesses based on your knowledge of
the story and of American life. Decide whether each answer is *likely* or *unlikely*.
Circle your choice. Then, working in small groups, give reasons for your choices
and discuss your opinions. There is no one correct answer, but there is more
evidence for some choices than for others.

1. Why did Garrison enjoy the trick played on Darla Ingqvist?

    a) He liked playing tricks, especially on the girls in the   *likely*   *unlikely*
        class.

    b) She deserved to be embarrassed more than any of the   *likely*   *unlikely*
        other students in class.

    c) He was glad Darla would finally notice him.   *likely*   *unlikely*

2. How do you think Garrison felt about the fact that the tree that they had
planted in the Arbor Day ceremony was killed in a softball game?

    a) He did not care. The game was more important than   *likely*   *unlikely*
        the tree.

    b) He felt guilty when he thought about Sylvester   *likely*   *unlikely*
        Krueger.

    c) He was glad somebody else had done it, so that he   *likely*   *unlikely*
        would not be punished by Mrs. Meyers.

6 | Retelling the Story

Use the phrases below and on page 48 to retell the story in your own words. As
you speak, try to include as many details as you can. A different student may
want to retell each part.

School started on the Tuesday after Labor
Day . . .

This information may help you:

- desks
- rooms
- floor wax
- portraits of Washington and
  Lincoln

- sympathetic
- a headache
- antique desk
- carved

Right on top of the desk it said . . .	• Sylvester Krueger '31 • brass plaque • "In memoriam"	• Mrs. Meyers • a lot to live up to
One time somebody put a big gob on the doorknob	• Darla Ingqvist • stuck-up • classroom monitor	• yank • Garrison was punished
On Arbor Day, the school had a ceremony . . .	• tree • Gettysburg Address • softball diamond	• stomped • a double

7 | Telling Your Own Stories

1 Find out which classmates have had the following experiences. Ask yes/no questions: for example, "Have you been strongly influenced by a hero?" Try to find one classmate for each statement. When you get a "yes" answer, write that classmate's name in the blank. Do not tell any stories yet. To begin the exercise, stand up and move around the classroom freely.

1. _____ has been strongly influenced by a hero.
   (name)

2. _____ remembers a special teacher from elementary or secondary
   (name)   school.

3. _____ remembers a trick that was played on someone in school.
   (name)

4. _____ was a hero at least once to the other children in school.
   (name)

2 Look at your list above. If several of you have stories for each experience, one of you should volunteer to be the storyteller. You can tell your stories to the whole class or to small groups. If almost everyone has a story to tell, you might want to work in pairs and exchange stories.

8 | *Getting into the Language*

A | *Notice the Structure: Present and Perfect Participles*

> "I was very excited when I saw Darla Ingqvist put her hand out, **knowing** what was on the doorknob."

The **boldface** word in the sentence above is a present participle. It is another way of saying, "*I knew* what was on the doorknob." In this kind of sentence, the verbs in clauses indicate actions that were happening more or less at the same time. The subject of the sentence appears in the main clause.

Present Participle (VERB + *-ing*)

I was very excited when I saw Darla Ingqvist put her hand out, **knowing** what was on the doorknob. **or**

Knowing what was on the doorknob, I was very excited when I saw Darla Ingqvist put her hand out.

> "I would begin to cry, for the shame of it, **having let down** this great hero."

In this sentence, the words in bold type are a perfect participle. It is another way of saying, "I *had let down* this great hero." The important thing to remember is that the second verb *(let down)* happened before the other one *(cry)*. Here, too, the subject of the sentence appears in the main clause.

Perfect Participle (*having* + **past participle**)

I would begin to cry, for the shame of it, **having let down** this great hero. **or**

Having let down this great hero, I would begin to cry, for the shame of it.

Practice the Structure

Read the following excerpt from Mrs. Meyers' journal. Then rewrite the
paragraphs, combining each pair of underlined sentences by changing each
asterisked (*) verb to a present or a perfect participle.

June 4, 1952

Well, the school year is almost over now and we're doing all of those year-end things that make me feel old. I monitored* the all-school picnic yesterday. Today I need a long rest. However, I truly enjoyed watching the boys and girls play together. The children were* in school all winter. They were very excited to be playing outside.

One of the last times I saw the whole school gathered outside was when we planted a tree on Arbor Day. It wasn't much of a tree, but it served our purpose. Yesterday, I watched* the children play softball. I worried the whole time about our little tree. The only place near the school that had good soil and enough water and light was, unfortunately, out in the middle of the softball diamond. The children finished almost the entire game without hitting the tree. Then, however, a boy moved* back to catch a ball. He stomped on the tree and broke it.

Some of the children were quite upset, especially little Darla Inggvist. But Garry Keillor soon hit a nice clean double and brought their attention back to the game. Afterwards, I cut off the rest of the tree. I remembered* my old student Sylvester Krueger. He was always such a good student. Good ballplayer too, if I remember correctly.

June 4, 1952

    Well, the school year is almost over now and we're doing all of those year-end things that make

me feel old. _____
1

_____.

However, I truly enjoyed watching the boys and girls play together. _____

_____.
2

One of the last times I saw the whole school gathered outside was when we planted a tree on Arbor Day. It wasn't much of a tree, but it served our purpose. _____.

3

The only place near the school that had good soil and enough water and light was, unfortunately, out in the middle of the softball diamond. The children finished almost the entire game without hitting the tree. _____.

4

Some of the children were quite upset, especially little Darla Ingqvist. But Gary Keillor soon hit a nice clean double and brought their attention back to the game. _____. He was

5

always such a good student. Good ballplayer too, if I remember correctly.

9 Extending the Story in Writing

A Writing Down a Story

Write down a story from Exercise 7, either one you heard or your own. If you choose another student's story, show your work to the storyteller when you finish. Ask the storyteller to comment on your version. Then revise the story, making any necessary changes and corrections.

B Writing a Personal Essay

In a personal essay, writers use their own experiences to illustrate points that others may be able to identify with. Because of the personal nature of the material, the first person is commonly used. Other than these differences, the structure is the same as that of any essay: an introduction containing a thesis statement, followed by several paragraphs of supporting material, and an ending with a brief conclusion.

Think of a hero or heroine and write a personal essay in which you discuss this person's life. Write your essay using Joseph Campbell's definitions. Professor Campbell spent his entire life studying the idea of the hero. He said:

> "A hero is someone who has given his or her life to something bigger than oneself." According to Professor Campbell, there are two kinds of heroic deeds: "one is the physical deed, in which a hero performs a courageous act in battle or saves a life. The other kind is the spiritual deed, in which the hero learns to experience the supernormal range of human spiritual life and then comes back with a message."

UNIT 5
The Lake Wobegon Cave

1 | Judging from Experience

Read the questions. Discuss the answers with your classmates.

1. Look at the drawing. What do you think the old man is saying to the boy?
2. Have you ever seen a cave? If so, what was it like?

Part One

A Vocabulary

Read the sentences and find the word or expression in the box that means the same as the italicized words. Then compare your answers with those of a classmate. If you disagree, consult another classmate, a dictionary or your teacher.

1. _____ Many men prefer to remain *bachelors* until they have begun to earn money and are able to help support a family.

2. _____ To make a clean, even cut in a piece of wood, you can put it on two *sawhorses.*

3. _____ Many people in Lake Wobegon own a home with several acres of *property.*

4. _____ The student was unable to complete her homework because she *was missing* her textbook.

5. _____ Children enjoy playing in the *woods.* They can create secret places under the trees and behind the thick bushes.

6. _____ The sound that a pig makes is a *grunt.*

7. _____ Most children learn to *crawl* before they stand up and walk.

8. _____ Some tourists prefer to take organized sightseeing trips, while others would rather *wander around* a new city alone.

9. _____ Limestone caves usually contain beautiful *stalagmites and stalactites.*

10. _____ In the summer, many people enjoy cooking meat on *skewers* over an open fire.

11. _____ After a building burns, people usually *block up* the windows and doors so that no one can get in.

a) close completely
b) move around with no plan
c) low short sound made deep in the throat
d) upward-pointing and downward-pointing rock formations
e) forest
f) unmarried men
g) land
h) long metal or wooden sticks
i) move on their hands and knees
j) could not find
k) movable frames for supporting wood

B Getting the Gist of the Story 🔲

This is a tall tale, a story that is difficult to believe. Mr. Haugen, an old family friend, tells young Paul Tollerud this story as they watch the other men build a new pig barn.

Listen to Part One of the story. Read the question and write your answer. Then compare your answer with those of your classmates.

How was the Lake Wobegon Cave discovered?

_____

_____

C Listening for Detail 🔲

Listen again to Part One. Decide whether each statement is true or false. Write *T* or *F* in the blank. Then compare your answers with those of a classmate. Listen again if you disagree with each other.

1. Mr. Haugen was helping to build the pig barn. _____

2. There is a cave on Grandpa Tollerud's property. _____

3. Great-grandpa Tollerud discovered the cave fifty years ago. _____

4. Great-grandpa Tollerud found the pigs because he could hear them. _____

5. Great-grandpa Tollerud did not go into the cave. _____

6. The pigs went into the cave because they were cold. _____

7. Most of the pigs did not want to leave the cave. _____

8. Great-grandpa Tollerud wanted his children to see the Lake Wobegon Cave. _____

Part Two

D Vocabulary

1 Read the sentences and find the word or expression in the box that means the same as the italicized words. Then compare your answers with those of a classmate. If you disagree, consult another classmate, a dictionary or your teacher.

1. _____ The Lake Wobegon pigs have two big curved *tusks* that they use for digging.

2. _____ The bottom floor of many houses is a cement *basement*.

3. _____ Many people enjoy *bacon* and eggs for breakfast.

4. _____ An earthquake may create *cracks* in the ground.

5. _____ At night, you can hear *creaks* in an old house, as if it were breathing.

6. _____ If parents suspect that a child is lying, they might say, *"There's more to this."*

7. _____ When a person tells a joke but does not smile, he might *wink* to let others know that he is not serious.

> **a)** thin openings caused by breaking
>
> **b)** underground part of a building
>
> **c)** open and close one eye rapidly
>
> **d)** This is more complex and significant.
>
> **e)** smoked meat from the back or sides of a pig
>
> **f)** long teeth that stick out of an animal's mouth
>
> **g)** sounds like those of a badly oiled door when it opens

2 Circle the letter of the expression that is closest in meaning to the italicized word or phrase. Then compare your answers with those of a classmate.

1. *It's hard to say* why people like to tell stories that frighten children.

   a) It's not clear   **b)** It's secret   **c)** It's obvious

2. The pressure of water in the ground can cause a floor to *bulge up*.

   a) smell   **b)** swell   **c)** shine

3. The dampness in basements often has a *rotten* smell.

   a) fragrant   **b)** sweet   **c)** unpleasant

4. The cave *runs* for miles along the hillside.

   a) jogs   **b)** continues   **c)** has water

5. Pigs like to *root around* in the dirt while they dig for food.

   a) sleep   **b)** play   **c)** search

6. Fire can be used to *scare away* a wild animal.

   a) frighten off   **b)** get away from   **c)** catch

E | Predicting and Listening

1 Working in small groups, discuss the question. Predict what might happen next in the story. Write down at least two possible answers.

What happened to the pigs that remained in the Lake Wobegon Cave?

a. _____

_____

b. _____

_____

c. _____

_____

2 Keeping your same groups, listen to the end of the story. Discuss how your predictions were different from the ending you heard.

F | Listening for Detail

Listen again to Part Two. Circle the letter of the answer that best completes each sentence. Then compare your answers with those of a classmate. Listen again if you disagree with each other.

1. According to Mr. Haugen, there are still pigs

   a) in the cave.

   b) downtown.

   c) in the woods.

2. Most of the pigs are

   a) pretty.

   b) dark.

   c) large.

3. The pigs try to get out by

   a) running.

   b) digging.

   c) eating.

4. According to Mr. Haugen, _____ in the basement prove that there are pigs underground.

   a) tusks

   b) dirt and dampness

   c) cracks

5. Mr. Haugen suggests that Paul's father goes down to the basement to _____ the pigs.

   a) scare away

   b) play with

   c) take care of

6. Paul asked his father, Daryl, if the story were true. Paul's grandfather, Carl, answered and said that it _____ true.

   a) was

   b) was not

   c) might be

3 | *Getting the Joke*

Read each item and decide which answer explains why the audience laughs. Circle
your choice. Then, working in groups, compare your answers. If you agree,
discuss the reasons for your choices. If you disagree, discuss your opinions and
try to come to an agreement. In each case, there is one choice that best explains
the joke.

1. "The boy said, 'How big do they get?'
   'Well, it's hard to say. Uh, the one I saw
   was pretty big, about the size of an
   elephant, actually.' "
   To Paul, pigs the size of elephants are
   frightening because they may

   a) eat a lot.

   b) weigh a lot.

   c) be living nearby.

2. " 'They're down there under the ground . . .
   and so they head for that smell of bacon
   frying,' he said. 'They head for the
   basement.' "
   One might not expect these pigs to enjoy
   the smell of bacon because

   a) bacon has a terrible odor.

   b) bacon is a form of pork.

   c) pigs do not like bacon.

3. "Does your dad ever go down into the
   basement, down there by himself, jump up
   and down and go, 'Ay, ya!'?"
   "Yea," the boy said, "yea."
   "That's what he's doing. He's scaring away
   those pigs."
   Rather than frightening pigs, it is more
   likely that Paul's father is

   a) expressing his frustration.

   b) singing.

   c) doing his exercises.

4. "Did you ever go down in your basement
   and smell a real rotten smell down there?
   That's pig breath."
   Since Americans consider pigs dirty, pig
   breath must be

   a) sweet.

   b) memorable.

   c) terrible.

4 Reviewing Vocabulary

Fill in each blank with one of these words or expressions. Be sure to use the
correct form of the italicized words. Compare your answers with those of a
classmate.

property	scare away	*creak*
run	*crawl*	it's hard to say
wink	*be* missing	*block* up
rotten	*wander* around	

While his father, Daryl, and his grandfather, Carl, were busy building a pig barn, Paul Tollerud sat

nearby, listening to old Mr. Haugen tell the story of the Lake Wobegon Cave. Mr. Haugen said that one

day seventy-five years ago, Paul's great-grandpa Tollerud _____ his pigs, so he
                                                                                    1

went in search of them all over his _____. While he was looking for them, he
                                                              2

found a large cave that _____ for miles under the town of Lake Wobegon. When
                                              3

he heard pig grunts coming from the cave, he _____ inside and saw that his pigs
                                                                      4

_____ among the stalactites and stalagmites. He got some of the pigs out, but many
              5

of them went farther back into the cave. After he left, he _____ the entrance to the
                                                                                  6

cave so that children would not go in.

Paul had a lot of questions to ask Mr. Haugen about the story. He wanted to know how big the pigs

were and if they ever escaped from the cave. When Paul asked about the size of the pigs, Mr. Haugen said,

"_____, since they only come out at night." He explained that
              7

_____ in Paul's house were actually the sounds of pigs trying to get out through the
              8

basement and that the _____ smell down there was pig breath. Mr. Haugen said
                                            9

that when Paul's father went down into the basement and yelled, he was actually trying to

_____ the pigs.
              10

When Paul asked his father whether the story were true or not, Mr. Haugen

_____, trying to get Paul's father to say "Yes." But he didn't. He asked his own
              11

father, Carl, who said that none of it was true.

5 Interpreting the Characters

Read the following questions and answers. The answers are not mentioned directly in the story, but it is possible to make good guesses based on your knowledge of the story and of American life. Decide whether each answer is *likely* or *unlikely*. Circle your choice. Then, working in small groups, give reasons for your choices and discuss your opinions. There is no one correct answer, but there is more evidence for some choices than for others.

1. Paul turned to his father, Daryl, and asked if the pig story were really true. Daryl caught old Mr. Haugen's wink and turned to ask his own father, Carl, the same question. Why did Daryl do this?

   a) Daryl remembered believing the story when he was a boy and did not want to frighten his son. *likely* *unlikely*

   b) Daryl wanted to find out if his own father, Carl, believed the story. *likely* *unlikely*

   c) Daryl did not want to show disrespect for Mr. Haugen and his story. *likely* *unlikely*

2. Why did Carl say that the story was not true?

   a) He thought Mr. Haugen was being cruel to Paul. *likely* *unlikely*

   b) He did not like tall tales. *likely* *unlikely*

   c) He wanted to end the conversation and go home. *likely* *unlikely*

Use these phrases to retell the story in your own words. As you speak, try to include as many details as you can. A different student may want to retell each part.

One afternoon when everyone was working on the pig barn, old Mr. Haugen began to talk to Paul, the youngest Tollerud boy . . .

This information may help you:

- sat on a sawhorse
- Great-grandpa Tollerud was missing his pigs
- found a cave
- heard pig grunts
- crawled down
- wandering around
- get warm
- got a few out, left the rest
- blocked up the entrance

Paul began to ask Mr. Haugen many questions . . .

- pigs there now
- size of the pigs
- pigs get out

Mr. Haugen asked Paul some questions . . .

- creaks at night
- father jumps up and down
- rotten smell in the basement

Paul began to doubt the story . . .

- Paul asked his father, Daryl
- Daryl looked at Mr. Haugen
- wink
- Daryl 30 years ago
- Daryl asked his father, Carl
- not a word
- Carl decided to go home
- not stop on the way

7 | *Telling Your Own Stories*

"The Lake Wobegon Cave" is a *tall tale,* a fantastic story invented to "explain" an ordinary phenomenon. Tall tales are often told to children to entertain them. "The Lake Wobegon Cave" tall tale "explains" why there are cracks and bad smells in people's basements.

Another type of story is the *fairy tale*. Such a story involves meetings between humans and magical creatures such as elves, fairies or dragons.

Legends are stories about people and places long ago, which cannot be proven, but which many people now accept as historical fact.

Myths are traditional stories that usually contain religious or magical ideas, and that often explain natural phenomena or historical events.

1 Find out which students have stories to tell by asking them whether they know a tall tale, fairy tale, legend or myth. Ask yes/no questions: for example, "Do you know a story from your country to tell the class?" Try to find at least four classmates who can tell a story. When you get a "yes" answer, write that classmate's name and the name of the country in the blanks. Do not tell any stories yet. To begin this exercise, stand up and move around the room freely.

1. _____ has a story from _____ to tell the class.
     (name)   (place)

2. _____ has a story from _____ to tell the class.
     (name)   (place)

3. _____ has a story from _____ to tell the class.
     (name)   (place)

4. _____ has a story from _____ to tell the class.
     (name)   (place)

Here is a list of stories. You might know one of them.

Africa and the Middle East	Asia
Aichia Khandicha	*Momotaro*
Chelm Stories	*The Story of Mooncakes*
Nasreddin	*Teja and Teji*
Scheherazade	*The Trickster Thief (Oriya)*
The Two Brothers	*Why the Sea is Salty*

Europe	The Americas
Baba Yaga	*La Tinette de Beurre*
Hansel and Gretel	*La Virgen de Guadalupe*
Heer Halewyn	*Patasola*
Lupomanaro	*Roba la gallina*
Loup Garrou	*Saciperere*

---

2 Look at your list above. If several of you have the same story to tell, one of you should volunteer to be the storyteller. You can tell your stories to the whole class or to small groups. If almost everyone has a story to tell, you might want to work in pairs and exchange stories.

8 Getting into the Language

A Notice the Structures: Direct and Indirect Speech

Mr. Haugen said, "Well, Paul, how are you doing?"

Paul said, "Oh, all right."

He said, "Paul, did you know that there's a cave on your grandpa's property?"

"The Lake Wobegon Cave" is a story told mostly in direct speech. In order to talk or write about the story, one can also use indirect speech. Many changes occur when moving from direct to indirect speech. Read these rules. Notice how they apply in the following statements and questions.

- The tense of the verb in direct speech usually changes when direct speech is reported as a past event in indirect speech: the present tense changes to past, and past and present perfect change to past perfect.
- Pronouns often change.
- The use of the word *that* to introduce indirect statements is optional.

Direct Statement	Indirect Statement
Paul replied, "Oh, **I am** all right."	Paul said **that he was** all right.
"**I have** never **seen** the cave," said Daryl.	Daryl said **he had** never **seen** the cave.
Mr. Haugen said, "Great-grandpa Tollerud **discovered** the cave."	Mr. Haugen said Great-grandpa Tollerud **had discovered** the cave.

- In indirect questions, question word order changes to statement word order.
- When introducing indirect *Wh-* questions, you cannot use the verb *say*. However, many different verbs can be used to introduce direct *Wh-* questions. For example, you can use *ask, say, wonder, explain, want to know, report.*

Direct *Wh-* Questions	Indirect *Wh-* Questions
The boy **said**, "What **do** they **eat**?"	The boy **asked** what they **ate**.
Paul asked, "When **did** Grandpa **lose** his pigs?"	Paul **wondered** when Grandpa **had lost** his pigs.
Paul **said**, "Why **is** the cave warm?"	Paul **asked** why the cave **was** warm.

- Direct yes/no questions can be introduced with many different verbs. Indirect questions are never introduced with the verb *say*. Indirect yes/no questions use either *if* or *whether*.

Direct Yes/No Questions	Indirect Yes/No Questions
Mr. Haugen **said,** "Paul, did your dad tell you about the cave?"	Mr. Haugen **asked** Paul **whether** his father had told him about the cave.
Paul wondered, "Are the pigs still down there?"	Paul **wondered if** the pigs were still down there.

B Practice the Structures

1 Read the dialog below. Complete the paragraph by changing each statement and question into indirect speech.

Direct Speech

Paul wondered, "How big do the pigs get?"

"I saw one the size of an elephant!" Mr. Haugen exclaimed.

Then Paul asked, "Can the pigs ever get out of the cave?"

Mr. Haugen answered, "Some are still there, but some have gotten out."

Paul then wanted to know, "How did they escape?"

Mr. Haugen replied, "They pushed up through somebody's basement."

Indirect Speech

Paul wondered how big the pigs got.

2 Read the paragraph below. Complete the paragraph by changing each indirect statement and question into direct speech.

Indirect Speech

Mr. Haugen asked if Paul heard creaks in the house at night. Paul said that he did. Then Mr. Haugen said that the creaks were signs of the pigs. Paul wondered how the pigs could breathe in the cave. Mr. Haugen answered that the rotten smell in his basement was caused by pig breath. Paul asked his father, Daryl, if the cave story were true. Paul's grandfather, Carl, answered that it was not.

Direct Speech

Mr. Haugen asked, "Paul, do you hear creaks in the house at night?"

9 Extending the Story in Writing

A Writing Down a Story

Write down a story from Exercise 7, either one you heard or your own. If you choose another student's story, show your work to the storyteller when you finish. Ask the storyteller to comment on your version. Then revise the story, making any necessary changes and corrections.

B Writing About What People Say

When writing down what people say, you have several choices. You can write exactly what they say, using direct speech. When you do this, you will have to incorporate some of the characteristics of the spoken language, such as idioms and slang expressions, contractions and hesitations. Or you can choose to use indirect speech. If you do this, you need to use the structures you studied in Exercise 8. Notice that when you use indirect speech, it is not necessary to report every word. Try to tell the gist of what people say.

Model

Mr. Haugen had told Paul the story of the Lake Wobegon cave to entertain him, but Paul's father felt that the story had frightened Paul. Paul's father believes that telling children frightening tales causes them unnecessary stress and fear. Imagine that Paul had a talk with his father later that same day. Compare these two models. The first is written in direct speech. The second is the same story written in indirect speech.

Direct Speech

Paul's father, Daryl, said, "I'd like to have a word with you, Son."

Paul answered, "OK, Dad."

Daryl asked, "Uh, why don't we go out on the porch?"

Paul replied, "Oh, OK."

Daryl wanted to know, "Listen, Paul, you remember that cave story Mr. Haugen told you today?"

Paul said, "Yeah . . ."

Daryl confided, "Well, my father told me that story, and it scared me, too."

Indirect Speech

Paul's father, Daryl, said to his son that he wanted to have a word with him. Paul agreed, so Daryl asked him to go out onto the porch with him, and he asked Paul if he remembered the cave story that Mr. Haugen had told him. With a little fear in his voice, Paul said that he did. So then Daryl confided that his own father had told him that same story, and that it had scared him, too.

Assignment

1. Continue the dialog between Daryl and Paul, using direct speech.

2. Look at either the dialog you have written or that of another classmate. Summarize the dialog as Daryl might for his wife. Use indirect speech, but remember that it is not necessary to include an indirect version of each and every line of the dialog. You might begin your summary like this:

After we finished with the pig barn today, I told Paul that I wanted to have a word with him out on the porch. . . .

UNIT 6
Thanksgiving: The Exiles Return

1 Judging from Experience

Read the questions. Discuss the answers with your classmates.

1. Look at the drawing. Why do you think that this woman is having so much trouble in the kitchen?
2. The last Thursday in November is circled on the wall calendar because it is Thanksgiving Day, an American national holiday. What do you know about this holiday? What are some of the traditional foods that are served on this day?

Part One

A Vocabulary

1 Circle the letter of the expression that is closest in meaning to the italicized word or phrase. Then compare your answers with those of a classmate.

1. People who smoke often have one last *drag* on a cigarette before they go into a no-smoking area.

   a) ash   **b)** inhalation   **c)** bite

2. When people go to a crowded restaurant, sometimes they go into the *lounge* and wait for a table.

   a) parking lot   **b)** kitchen   **c)** bar

3. If a person smokes cigarettes or eats strong food, he or she might use a *breath mint* to cover the smell.

   a) fresh-tasting candy   **b)** deodorant   **c)** perfume

4. People usually try to get everything *shined up* around their homes before their guests arrive for a holiday celebration.

   a) arranged neatly on shelves   **b)** cleaned and polished   **c)** hidden

5. All year long, many families in the U.S. *get along on* simple foods, but on Thanksgiving the food must be very special.

   a) like   **b)** buy   **c)** manage on

6. A very easy kind of meal can be made by cutting up some vegetables and meat, adding some liquid, and cooking it all in a *casserole* in the oven.

   a) frying pan   **b)** covered baking dish   **c)** pot

7. If the table at a big family dinner is too small, everybody can *scooch* together a little bit.

   a) push   **b)** eat   **c)** talk

2 Read the sentences and find the word or expression in the box that means the same as the italicized words. Then compare your answers with those of a classmate. If you disagree, consult another classmate, a dictionary or your teacher.

1. _____ *Pâté* made from goose liver is very tasty.

2. _____ The family bought a new *coffee table* to put in front of the living room sofa.

3. _____ When you have guests, you try to *do what is right by them.*

4. _____ When the cook was squeezing an orange, some juice *squirted* into her eye.

5. _____ It is not a good idea to *try out* a new recipe when you are having guests for dinner.

6. _____ To make it easier to eat, cooks sometimes *debone* meat before serving it.

7. _____ Sometimes cooks make a *dressing* and stuff it inside a chicken or a turkey before they cook it.

8. _____ There was no traffic this morning, so I made it from home to the office in 45 minutes *flat.*

9. _____ Trying to make a complicated new dish for dinner can be a *harrowing* experience.

10. _____ When some people are angry, they *curse under their breath* because they do not want others to hear what they are saying.

11. _____ A *head-on collision* on the highway is a very frightening thing.

12. _____ Because there was no room in the closet, all the guests' coats were lying in a *heap* on the bed.

a) remove the bones from

b) exactly

c) sprayed

d) honor them by doing the appropriate thing

e) painful, difficult

f) small, low table

g) experiment with

h) disorganized pile

i) crash involving two motor vehicles, front to front

j) a mixture of spices and bread or rice

k) food made by crushing solid foods into a soft, smooth mass

l) swear in a low voice

3 Read the recipes and find the expression in the box that means the same as the underlined words. Then compare your answers with those of a classmate. If you disagree, consult another classmate, a dictionary or your teacher.

1. _a_

2. _____

3. _____

4. _____

5. _____

6. _____

7. _____

8. _____

9. _____

Mabel Tollefson's Tuna Fish Casserole

Combine in a mixing bowl:
1 9-oz. can tuna fish
1 10-oz. can mushroom soup
1 10-oz. can peas, without liquid
1/2 cup milk
1/2 cup grated cheese
Place in a greased casserole.
Top with a mixture of:
1/3 cup grated cheese
1/3 cup breadcrumbs
Bake at 350° for 30-40 minutes

Mabel Tollefson's E-Z Party Meat Hors D'oeuvres

Weiners on sticks
Fry or broil:
1 package of 8 to 12 weiners
Cut into 1/2-inch lengths, and serve either hot or cold with colored toothpicks and small dishes of tomato catsup or mustard.

Liverwurst on Ritz crackers
Slice 1 12-oz. liverwurst into 1/2-inch lengths, then cut into quarters, each about 1-inch square. Place a square on each cracker.

Arlene Bunsen's Tasty Meat Loaf

Combine in a large mixing bowl:
1 lb. ground beef
1 chopped onion
1 chopped green pepper
1 egg
1/2 cup tomato catsup
1 tablespoon mustard
1 cup broken crackers
Place in a greased loaf pan and bake at 350° for 1 hour.

Virginia Ingqvist's Hamburger Hot Dish

Brown in a frying pan:
1 lb. ground beef
1 medium onion, chopped
Drain grease. Remove from heat.
Mix in a large casserole:
1 large green pepper, chopped
4 large carrots, chopped
2 cups egg noodles, dry
1 10-oz. can mushroom soup
salt, pepper, parsley, to taste
Mix in onions and meat. Bake at 325° for 1 hour.

a) a soft liver sausage

b) a small, thin, bread-like cake

c) hot dogs, the most typical American sausage

d) the flesh of a common large sea fish; usually sold ready-cooked in cans

e) ground beef

f) ground meat mixed with other ingredients and formed into a bread-like shape

g) a heated kind of food, usually the main part of a meal

h) the brand name for a kind of cracker, taken from the name of a very famous and expensive hotel

i) very small portions of food served before the meal

B | Getting the Gist of the Story

The first Thanksgiving was celebrated by the Pilgrims in the year 1621. It has become one of the most important family days. Thanksgiving is a time when people travel long distances to celebrate together.

This is a story about three families in Lake Wobegon—the Tollefsons, the Ingqvists and the Bunsens—and what happened when their grown children and grandchildren came home for Thanksgiving. Garrison calls these children "exiles," as if they had been forced to leave home and are finally returning after a long absence.

Listen to Part One of the story. Read the question and write your answer. Then compare your answer with those of your classmates.

The Tollefsons and the Ingqvists were getting ready for the arrival of their children. What kind of general activity was going on at these two homes?

C | Listening for Detail

Listen again to Part One. Circle the letter of the answer that best completes each sentence. Then compare your answers with those of a classmate. Listen again if you disagree with each other.

1. For the returning children, the town of Lake Wobegon

   a) seems new and interesting.

   b) is painful to look at.

   c) has not changed very much.

2. The returning children behaved as if they were

   a) frequent visitors.

   b) twelve years old.

   c) not interested in being there.

3. Many of the adult children who grew up in Lake Wobegon drive home for Thanksgiving. They now live

   a) in cities.

   b) about ten miles down the road.

   c) downtown.

4. At the Tollefson home, the hors d'oeuvres were made for

   a) the dog.

   b) Claudia Tollefson and her husband, Todd.

   c) Mom and Dad.

5. Virginia Ingqvist tried out a new recipe that involved pulling the skin from the turkey and then

   a) putting it back.

   b) throwing it away.

   c) twisting it with a knife.

6. When Virginia took a look at the turkey in the oven, she

   a) fell apart.

   b) did not recognize it.

   c) saw a big heap.

Part Two

D Vocabulary

1 Circle the letter of the expression that is closest in meaning to the italicized word or phrase. Then compare your answers with those of a classmate. If you disagree, consult another classmate, a dictionary or your teacher.

1. Despite all her troubles in the kitchen, Virginia Ingqvist did not feel like a failure. She was *a valiant* woman.

   a) an intelligent   **b)** a valuable   **c)** a brave

2. It is difficult to cut animal bones or some foods such as coconuts. You have to *whack* them with a big, heavy knife.

   a) slowly divide   **b)** carefully cut   **c)** forcefully hit

3. Some people do not use recipes when they cook—they just *dump* the ingredients together and hope that the meal will taste good.

   a) add without measuring   **b)** carefully mix   **c)** slowly stir

4. After a big dinner, people often say that the dining room and the kitchen are filled with "*wreckage*," as if there had been a disaster.

   a) broken plates   **b)** dirty dishes   **c)** people

5. Creative cooks often simply use whatever spices are *close at hand*.

   a) in their hands   **b)** nearby   **c)** in the recipe

6. The day before the dinner party, four people said they could not come. The host was *just as glad* that they could not come, since a smaller party is less work than a larger one.

   a) happy   **b)** unhappy   **c)** worried

7. Some people say exactly what they are thinking; but if a statement is too direct, it can sound *blunt*.

   a) rough   **b)** boring   **c)** surprising

8. If you talk about a difficult personal problem at the dinner table, family members may lift their eyes and *stare at* you, not knowing what to say.

   a) wait for   **b)** look directly at   **c)** speak to

9. After drying the dishes, the man put them where they *went*.

   a) are used   **b)** are washed   **c)** are stored

10. After dinner, the table should be cleared and *wiped off* with a wet cloth.

   a) cleaned   **b)** put away   **c)** set

2 Find the expression in the box that means the same as the numbered items in the picture. Then compare your answers with those of a classmate.

1. _e_ china cabinet
7. _____ cabin
2. _____ platter
6. _____ plaster centerpiece
5. _____ sherry
3. _____ sieve
4. _____ gravy boat

a) a strong kind of wine, originally from Spain

b) a small, deep long-shaped container with a handle for serving meat juices

c) a decoration placed in the middle of a table, here one made of a hard white material that is made from water, sand and lime (CaO)

d) a kitchen tool with holes, used for separating solid things from liquid

e) a cupboard, often with glass doors, where fine dishes and glasses are stored

f) a small, roughly built house

g) a large flat dish

E Predicting and Listening

1 Working in small groups. discuss the question. Predict what might happen next in the story. Write down at least two possible answers.

When Virginia Ingqvist looked at her turkey creation in the oven, it had all fallen apart. What do you think she decided to serve for Thanksgiving dinner?

a. _____

b. _____

c. _____

2 Keeping your same groups, listen to the end of the story. Discuss how your predictions were different from the ending you heard.

F Listening for Detail

Listen again to Part Two. Circle the letter of the answer that best completes each sentence. Then compare your answers with those of a classmate. Listen again if you disagree with each other.

1. Virginia Ingqvist made a turkey

   a) soup.

   b) casserole.

   c) sandwich.

2. At the home of Arlene Bunsen, they ate a

   _____ turkey.

   a) baked

   b) boiled

   c) fried

3. The last time that Barbara Ann Bunsen had been in the kitchen with her mother was

   _____ ago.

   a) an hour

   b) a long time

   c) a year

4. According to Garrison, it is easier to talk in the kitchen than at the dinner table because in the kitchen you are

   a) tired.

   b) not hungry.

   c) busy working.

5. Arlene Bunsen told her daughter Barbara Ann that she felt _____ her.

   a) proud of

   b) angry at

   c) disappointed with

6. Barbara Ann was surprised that

   a) her mother started to sing.

   b) there were so many dishes.

   c) she knew where the dishes went.

7. Barbara Ann put the plaster Pilgrim centerpiece

   a) on the table.

   b) in the china cabinet.

   c) in the sink.

3 | *Getting the Joke*

Read each item and decide which answer explains why the audience laughs. Circle your choice. Then, working in groups, compare your answers. If you agree, discuss the reasons for your choices. If you disagree, discuss your opinions and try to come to an agreement. In each case, there is one choice that best explains the joke.

1. "A lot of homes that had gotten along on tuna fish casserole and meat loaf and hamburger hot dish were doing some pretty fancy cooking this last week. They had hors d'oeuvres at the Tollefsons' for Thanksgiving. Hors d'oeuvres, if you can believe it."

   Hors d'oeuvres are served before sitting down to formal dinners. Since the Tollefsons usually eat tuna fish, meat loaf and hamburger, having hors d'oeuvres is

   a) an unpleasant change.

   b) an amusing surprise.

   c) a big mistake.

2. "Food on the coffee table had never been seen in that home before. Their dog was kind of surprised by it. Figured it was for him. Had a little bit of it, but of course it wasn't."

   The Tollefsons' dog was surprised because there was food

   a) in a new place.

   b) for him.

   c) on sticks.

3. "The hors d'oeuvres were for Claudia and for her husband, Todd, who drove up from Chicago, where they are quite active in the arts. Mom and Dad wanted to do what was right by them."

   People who appreciate dance, music, painting and so on usually expect to eat

   _____ food.

   a) common

   b) unusual

   c) frozen

4. "Virginia Ingqvist, for the turkey this year, tried out a new recipe which she had seen a woman do on *Good Morning, America* in about 45 seconds flat."

   Television cooks such as the one Virginia saw usually

   a) do not eat what they make.

   b) make complicated foods.

   c) forget something.

5. "The turkey looked as if it had been in a head-on collision with something."

Virginia's turkey looked as if it had been in a bad auto accident because it was

a) covered with grease.

b) on fire.

c) completely destroyed.

6. "Virginia threw the turkey back in the oven, cooked it for another hour, brought it out and served it in bowls."

A turkey is usually cooked whole and carved into slices at the table. The kind of food that is usually served in bowls is

a) hot.

b) cold.

c) liquid.

7. "The gravy boat went up behind the cereal boxes."

The gravy boat is probably used

a) very carefully.

b) very rarely.

c) every weekend.

8. "The little centerpiece, the little plaster Pilgrims standing by their plaster cabin with the plaster pine tree and the plaster smoke coming out of the chimney, was wiped off with a damp cloth and put away in the china cabinet until next year."

Barbara Ann and her family feel that the Pilgrim centerpiece is very important to their holiday celebration. This representation of Pilgrim life is

a) historically accurate.

b) stereotypical.

c) ridiculous.

4 Reviewing Vocabulary

Fill in each blank with one of these words or expressions. Be sure to use the correct form of the italicized words. Then compare your answers with those of a classmate.

get along on	*try* out	valiant	*curse* under *one's* breath
be just as glad	shined up	*go*	flat
wipe off	hors d'oeuvres	harrowing	close at hand

It was Thanksgiving in Lake Wobegon last week, so all of the children who had grown up and moved away were coming back to celebrate the holiday with their families. There was a great deal of housecleaning and cooking as people got their houses _____ in preparation for their children's return. Those who _____ plain meals were looking forward to the holiday.

At the Tollefson's house, they welcomed their children home with _____ on the coffee table. These were prepared especially for Todd and Claudia, who live in Chicago and are active in the arts.

At the Ingqvists' home, Virginia _____ a new turkey recipe that she had seen someone demonstrate on TV in 45 seconds _____. When she attempted it, it was a _____ experience: the turkey fell apart in the oven. However, Virginia was a _____ woman. She took the wrecked turkey out of the oven, and desperately tried to improve it. Upset and in a hurry, Virginia added whatever spices were _____. She was _____ the entire time. In the end, she served the turkey in bowls.

At the Bunsen house, they ate a traditional roast turkey. Afterwards, Barbara Ann and her mother cleaned everything up. Barbara Ann _____ that nobody else had offered to help, because she wanted to work and talk with her mother alone in the kitchen. Arlene washed and Barbara Ann dried. Barbara Ann was surprised to know that even though she did not live at home any longer, she still remembered where everything _____, including the Pilgrim centerpiece. She _____ this little plaster sculpture with a damp cloth and put it away in the cabinet until next year.

5 | *Interpreting the Characters*

Read the following questions and answers. The answers are not mentioned directly in the story, but it is possible to make good guesses based on your knowledge of the story and of American life. Decide whether each answer is *likely* or *unlikely*. Circle your choice. Then, working in small groups, give reasons for your choices and discuss your opinions. There is no one correct answer, but there is more evidence for some choices than for others.

1. Some of the returning exiles stopped at the Crossroads Lounge, a bar outside of Lake Wobegon, for a last drink before they arrived home. Why did they do this?

    a) Their parents did not have the right kinds of alcohol   *likely*   *unlikely*
    at home.

    b) They were nervous about going home and wanted a   *likely*   *unlikely*
    drink to calm down.

    c) Their parents did not approve of drinking alcohol.   *likely*   *unlikely*

2. Mr. and Mrs. Tollefson served hors d'oeuvres for the first time this Thanksgiving. Why did they do this?

    a) Their daughter Claudia and her husband, Todd, are   *likely*   *unlikely*
    sophisticated city people who expect to have fancy
    food.

    b) They wanted to use their new coffee table.   *likely*   *unlikely*

    c) Because they had just arrived from Chicago, Claudia   *likely*   *unlikely*
    and Todd needed something light to eat before the
    main meal.

3. Barbara Ann helped her mother, Arlene, clean up the kitchen after Thanksgiving dinner. Why was she glad that nobody else offered to help?

    a) She wanted to be alone with her mother and hoped   *likely*   *unlikely*
    that they could have a personal talk.

    b) She wanted to test herself and see whether she   *likely*   *unlikely*
    remembered where everything in the kitchen went.

    c) A third person in the kitchen would have made it too   *likely*   *unlikely*
    crowded.

6 | Retelling the Story

Use these phrases to retell the story in your own words. As you speak, try to include as many details as you can. A different student may want to retell each part.

This information may help you:

A lot of children and grandchildren returned home to Lake Wobegon for Thanksgiving . . .

- family holiday
- exiles
- from the city
- stopped at the Crossroads Lounge
- last drag on a cigarette
- breath mints

It was a busy week of cleaning and cooking. At the Tollefsons' house, they . . .

- hors d'oeuvres
- the dog
- Claudia and Todd from Chicago
- active in the arts

At the Ingqvists', Virginia tried a new recipe for turkey . . .

- *Good Morning, America*
- harrowing experience
- head-on collision
- casserole dish
- spices and sherry
- bowls

At the Bunsens', they had a traditional Thanksgiving meal. Afterwards, Barbara Ann and her mother, Arlene, . . .

- worked in the kitchen
- talking together
- little announcements
- proud of you
- where things went
- wiped off plaster Pilgrim centerpiece

7 | Telling Your Own Stories

1 Find out which classmates have had the following experiences. Ask yes/no questions: for example, "Have you ever tried to hide some bad behavior from your parents?" Try to find one classmate for each statement. When you get a "yes" answer, write that classmate's name in the blank. Do not tell any stories yet. To begin the exercise, stand up and move around the classroom freely.

1. _____ has tried to hide some bad behavior from his or her parents.
   (name)

2. _____ has had a disaster in the kitchen.
   (name)

3. _____ has gone home after a long absence.
   (name)

4. _____ has an important object that is used only on a special
   (name)   holiday.

2 Look at your list above. If several of you have stories for each experience, one
   of you should volunteer to be the storyteller. You can tell your stories to the
   whole class or to small groups. If almost everyone has a story to tell, you
   might want to work in pairs and exchange stories.

8 Getting into the Language

A Notice the Structures: Past Perfect—Active and Passive Forms

---

"Homes that **had gotten along** on tuna casserole and meat loaf and hamburger
hot dish were doing some pretty fancy cooking here this last week."

The past perfect active form refers to an action that came before another action or
event in the past. In the example above, "homes had gotten along on" simple
home-cooked meals until "last week," when fancy cooking started.

Past Perfect Active Form

had + past participle   Before Thanksgiving dinner, the family **had
                           worked** for days to get the house all shined up.

"Food on the coffee table **had never been seen** in that home before."

The example above is also in the past perfect tense, but it is passive. Before this
year's Thanksgiving celebration, the coffee table had not been used to serve food.

Past Perfect Passive Form

had + *been* + past participle   The silver **had been polished,** the table
                                    had been waxed and the whole house **had
                                    been cleaned.**

B | *Practice the Structures*

1 Listen again to Part Two of the story, or read the Tapescript, and try to find four other examples of the past perfect tense. Write the sentences here. Then compare your answers with those of a classmate.

Barbara Ann was just as glad that . . .

_____

_____

_____

2 Thank-you notes are short letters to express gratitude for a gift or a pleasant social occasion. In a thank-you note, you usually mention the special character of the gift or the event, such as its usefulness, beauty or pleasantness, and you acknowledge the special efforts or thoughtfulness of the person.

    Read the two notes and fill in the blanks with the past perfect form of the verbs in parentheses. Use active and passive forms, as appropriate.

a. If you do not know the person who gave the party or the gift, the language in the thank-you note will be formal. This note is from a woman who was invited for Thanksgiving to the Tollefson home. As a friend of Claudia and Todd's in Chicago, she had never met Claudia's parents before. Therefore, her note is formal.

November 30th

Dear Mr. and Mrs. Tollefson,

    I want to thank you for the wonderful meal you prepared last week and for the warmth of your hospitality. As Claudia told you, my family lives far away, so it is difficult for me to go home for Thanksgiving.

    Before we arrived, Claudia _____ (1. tell) me that you enjoy Thanksgiving more than any other holiday. Everything certainly did look as if it _____ (2. prepare) with great care-- the flowers, the table and, of course, the meal.

    Thank you again for the wonderful time. I felt very welcomed.

                       Sincerely,

                       Emily Crane

---

b. If you know the person who gave the party or the gift, the language in your thank-you note will be very informal. Here is the note that Todd wrote to his in-laws.

December 6th

Dear Mabel and Ted,

Thanksgiving was great! Before we arrived, Claudia _____ (1. warn) me that there would be more of a crowd than usual, but I _____ not _____ (2. expect) thirty people! I don't know how you managed to get things shined up for so many guests. Knowing you, though, you probably just shoved everything in the closets and under the beds in half an hour flat.

And thanks for making room at the last minute for our friend Emily. She _____ not _____ (3. have) anyplace to go for Thanksgiving for the past couple of years, so I know that she appreciated it. On the ride back to the city, she said that she knew that everything _____ (4. fix) with a lot of love. I know what she means. By the way, I think that she kind of liked having to scooch close to cousin Lars on the piano bench at dinner! What did he say about her later? Well, I've got to go now. Take care.

Love to you both,
Todd

9 Extending the Story in Writing

A Writing Down a Story

Write down a story from Exercise 7, either one you heard or your own. If you choose another student's story, show your work to the storyteller when you finish. Ask the storyteller to comment on your version. Then revise the story, making any necessary changes and corrections.

B Writing a Recipe

Model

Virginia Ingqvist tried out a new recipe this year for her Thanksgiving turkey. It was a disaster, so she had to invent a new recipe in order to save the meal. However, at the Bunsen home, they had their turkey cooked the normal way. Following is a recipe for a traditional Thanksgiving turkey, along with a recipe for one kind of dressing that can be cooked inside of the turkey.

David's Roast Turkey with Fruit and Nut Dressing   (serves 15-18)

Clean and remove the neck from:

one 12-15 lb. turkey

Wash the turkey in cold water and gently pat it dry. Sprinkle it inside with:

salt and pepper, according to your taste.

Stuff the turkey with **dressing** (see dressing recipe).

Close the opening, bend the wings backwards under the bird, place it breast side up in a shallow roasting pan, and brush with:

1/3 cup melted butter

Bake at 325° Fahrenheit, occasionally brushing with its own juices, for about 4 to 4 1/2 hours, or until the juice runs clear, not bloody, when the joint between the leg and the body is pierced with a knife.

David's Fruit and Nut Turkey Dressing   (for one 12-15 lb. turkey)

In a large saucepan, slowly melt:

1/4 cup butter

Add and gently heat:

1/2 cup chopped onion
1/2 cup chopped celery
1/2 cup raisins or other dried fruit
1/2 cup chopped pistachios or other nuts

Heat this mixture until the onions become soft, but not browned. Remove from heat. In a mixing bowl, combine:

2 eggs, beaten
2 tablespoons of chopped parsley
1 teaspoon of coriander powder
1 teaspoon of sage powder
6 cups of breadcrumbs

Add the bread and spice mixture to the cooked vegetables. Mix thoroughly and stuff the turkey cavity. Do not stuff too tightly.

Assignment

Think of a favorite holiday recipe and write it down, using either the American system of weights and measures or the metric system. Be sure to include all the necessary ingredients, with measurements. Also write down all the steps required to prepare the dish. Make the recipe clear enough so a classmate can use it.

If you cannot write such a recipe from memory, talk with other students in your class who might know how to make this dish, or visit the library or a bookstore to find more information. You might want to talk to your classmates, collect recipes and then prepare a meal for the class.

UNIT 7
Father Emil's Starry Night

1 Judging from Experience

Read the questions. Discuss the answers with your classmates.

1. Look at the drawing. What kind of programs do you suppose the children are watching on TV?
2. What do you imagine this old man is thinking?

Part One

A Vocabulary

1 Read the sentences and find the word or expression in the box that means the same as the italicized words. Then compare your answers with those of a classmate. If you disagree, consult another classmate, a dictionary or your teacher.

1. _____ Roses can be many colors: white, yellow, pink or *crimson*.

2. _____ *Satellite TV dishes* provide good, clear pictures for people who live far from a city.

3. _____ Sometimes mountains or tall buildings can cause bad television *reception*.

4. _____ A priest often lives right next door to the church, in the *rectory*.

5. _____ The advantage of using a credit card to buy something expensive is that you can *pay* it *off* slowly.

6. _____ When you go to a new country, everything can seem very *odd;* nothing feels familiar or comfortable.

7. _____ Sometimes very violent prisoners are kept separate from the others in *solitary confinement*.

8. _____ Coca Cola and Pepsi Cola are two very popular kinds of *pop*.

9. _____ Not all men in the religious professions are priests; some are *monks*.

10. _____ We knew that he had problems, but he never shared them with anyone; he just *brooded* about them.

a) picture and sound quality

b) buy with a series of payments

c) devices that receive signals from a man-made object that circles the earth in space

d) strange

e) soda, soft drink

f) dark red

g) house for a priest

h) worried silently

i) alone in special jail cells

j) members of an all-male religious community who live and work together

2 Circle the letter of the expression that is closest in meaning to the italicized word or phrase. Then compare your answers with those of a classmate.

1. For over twenty minutes, the salesman successfully *latched on to* a customer who did not seem to be interested in the product.

   a) refused to let go of   **b)** watched over   **c)** thought about

2. Few people have the time to read the entire newspaper; most of us simply *skim* the articles that interest us.

   a) cut out   **b)** look quickly at   **c)** misunderstand

3. In Southern California, which has a semi-desert climate, the sky is rarely *overcast*.

   a) filled with stars   **b)** blue   **c)** dark with clouds

4. Many people are *leery of* salespeople. They are afraid that a salesperson will convince them to buy something that they really do not need.

   a) bored by   **b)** interested in   **c)** suspicious of

5. A large number of people were *impoverished* after the war. They could not even buy bread.

   a) made poor   **b)** made sad   **c)** made curious

6. When the popular rock star came out on the stage, the crowd *went bananas*.

   a) left the theater   **b)** became very excited   **c)** threw fruit

7. When a person has been sick for a long time, his or her skin becomes *sallow*.

   a) discolored   **b)** painful   **c)** dry

8. Some people are so sensitive that they cannot *bear* seeing anything unpleasant.

   a) avoid   **b)** remember   **c)** tolerate

B Getting the Gist of the Story 📼

This is a story about Father Emil, the Catholic priest in Lake Wobegon. We hear about a plan he has for the young people in town, and then we hear about Emil when he was a young man.

Listen to Part One of the story. Read the questions and write your answers. Then compare your answers with those of your classmates.

1. What did Father Emil think about buying for the church Youth Center?

_____

2. What was the reason for his final decision?

_____

C Listening for Detail

Listen again to Part One. Circle the letter of the answer that best completes each sentence. Then compare your answers with those of a classmate. Listen again if you disagree with each other.

1. Father Emil talked with the satellite TV dish salesman because he wanted to

   a) read the sales literature.

   b) make money for the church.

   c) attract young people to the church.

2. When the salesman showed Father Emil the satellite TV dish brochure, he

   a) showed all of the pictures.

   b) took several pictures.

   c) covered up some pictures.

3. Father Emil decided that most television programs are not made in Minnesota, since

   a) Minnesota is too cold.

   b) it is never cloudy or snowy on TV.

   c) Minnesota is so odd.

4. Father Emil wondered why people on television get excited

   a) about coffee.

   b) about being poor.

   c) over bananas.

5. Father Emil's brother offered to

   a) visit him.

   b) buy him a TV set.

   c) live in Lake Wobegon.

6. Emil's father had always had bad luck farming, so he

   a) sold the farm.

   b) gave the farm to Emil.

   c) sold the furniture.

7. Emil's father had bad luck and almost never

   a) smoked.

   b) spoke.

   c) brooded.

8. After Emil helped his father load the truck, they both

   a) counted the stars.

   b) looked for a tree.

   c) smoked cigarettes.

9. As Emil and his father stood outside their house in western North Dakota, they could see

   a) many trees.

   b) many houses.

   c) millions of stars.

Part Two

D Vocabulary

Read the sentences and find the word or expression in the box that means the same as the italicized words. Then compare your answers with those of a classmate. If you disagree, consult another classmate, a dictionary or your teacher.

1. _____ *It's about time* for us to go home; we have a long trip, and it's very late.

2. _____ Children grow up, leave home and then try to *make something of themselves.*

3. _____ It is very exciting to *start out* on a journey or a new job.

4. _____ Some people prefer to work together; others prefer to work *on their own.*

5. _____ It is illegal to *hitchhike* in many parts of the U.S.; drivers who pick up people along the road are often stopped by the police.

6. _____ A *monastery* is usually far away from the rest of the world and its problems.

7. _____ A two-year-old child usually has an unsteady *gait,* but soon the child can move as well as an adult.

8. _____ Athletes often develop a *limp* after receiving a leg or a foot injury.

9. _____ At a wedding party, the musicians will often play a *waltz* for the guests.

10. _____ At a wedding, the bride often wears a white *veil.*

11. _____ At the end of a wedding, the priest gives a final *blessing* to the bride and groom.

a) place where monks live and work

b) it is the right moment

c) travel by getting rides in strangers' cars

d) work to develop a career

e) begin

f) alone, independently

g) thin cloth used to cover the face and/or head

h) prayer

i) style of walking

j) obvious weakness in the leg when walking

k) dance whose steps are done in groups of three: 1-2-3, 1-2-3

E Predicting and Listening

1 Working in small groups. discuss the question. Predict what might happen next in the story. Write down at least two possible answers.

During the Great Depression, from 1929 to the end of the 1930s, the world economy collapsed and millions of people lost their jobs and their homes. In the U.S., a lack of rain for many years made the situation worse for farmers. Dry winds blew the soil away, and many farmers were forced to leave home and look for work.

On a starry night in 1931, Emil and his father stood out by the family truck the evening before they were planning to move west to California. Emil felt that his father was about to talk to him. What do you think Emil's father was going to say?

a. _____

b. _____

c. _____

2   Keeping your same groups, listen to the end of the story. Discuss how your predictions were different from the ending you heard.

F   *Listening for Detail*

Listen again to Part Two. Decide whether each statement is true or false. Write *T* or *F* in the blank. Then compare your answers with those of a classmate. Listen again if you disagree with each other.

1. Emil left the day after his father spoke to him. _____

2. Emil slept outdoors for three days. _____

3. Emil decided to live at a monastery. _____

4. Father Emil goes out even on the coldest evenings of the winter. _____

5. Because he is old now and has a limp, Father Emil does not like

   to walk. _____

6. Some of the houses in Lake Wobegon are decorated with blue lights

   at night. _____

7. The people in the houses do not know that Father Emil is outside. _____

8. Father Emil cannot remember the names of all of the children in Lake

   Wobegon. _____

3 | *Getting the Joke*

Read each item and decide which answer explains why the audience laughs. Circle your choice. Then, working in groups, compare your answers. If you agree, discuss the reasons for your choices. If you disagree, discuss your opinions and try to come to an agreement. In each case, there is one choice that best explains the joke.

1. "But then the salesman showed him the brochure that described the channels and the programs that you'd get with a satellite TV dish. And he kind of skimmed over a few pages real fast, and he sort of put his hand over some of the photographs."
   The salesman was afraid that if Father Emil knew about the sex and violence that one can see on satellite channels, Father Emil would

   a) be embarrassed.

   b) not buy a satellite TV dish.

   c) start to give a talk on morality.

2. "It almost never snows on television. There are almost no cloudy, overcast days. Television isn't made in Minnesota, evidently; comes from someplace else."
   Garrison is suggesting that life on TV is

   a) beautiful.

   b) very colorful.

   c) not realistic.

3. "The people in the commercials are so odd. How excited they get about a new detergent, or a cup of coffee; it's as if they're impoverished, as if they'd been in solitary confinement for years, so that they get this particular bottle of pop, and they just go bananas over it."
   The things that people on commercials get very excited about are

   a) valuable.

   b) ordinary.

   c) important.

4. "Father Emil has a slight limp, so when he walks, it's almost like a waltz. He goes 'ttch-TTCH, ttch-TTCH, ttch-TTCH, ttch-TTCH.' Not that fast, that's downhill."
   When Father Emil walks uphill, he has only a slight limp. But when he goes downhill, his gait makes it seem like he is

   a) dancing.

   b) running.

   c) slowing down.

4 | *Reviewing Vocabulary*

Fill in each blank with one of these words or expressions. Be sure to use the correct form of the italicized words. Compare your answers with those of a classmate.

go bananas	make something of *oneself*	it *be* about time
leery of	bear	*skim*
monk	pay off	*latch* on to
start out	odd	*brood*

    Recently, a satellite TV dish salesman came to Lake Wobegon. Father Emil was interested, so he

_____ the salesman for quite a while. He thought that with a satellite dish, he
$\qquad$ 1

would get clear TV reception, and he could attract children to the church Youth Center. If he charged them

a fee to watch, he could _____ the cost of the dish quickly. The salesman knew,
$\qquad$ 2

however, that a priest would not like some of the programs available, so he _____
$\qquad$ 3

over a few pages in the brochure very fast.

    But that is not why Father Emil decided not to get a satellite TV dish. He has always been

_____ TV, probably because the people on TV and their emotions seem so
$\qquad$ 4

exaggerated and unnatural. They are so _____. For example, he does not trust the
$\qquad$ 5

way that the people in commercials _____ over the simplest products like coffee or
$\qquad$ 6

soda or detergent. When Emil's brother wanted to buy him a TV, Emil said that he did not want one. He

said that he would rather live a simple life, like a _____.
$\qquad$ 7

    When he was young, Emil's family lost their farm in the Great Depression. His father was a sad man

who _____ about his hard life. He had the kind of sickly face and empty eyes that
$\qquad$ 8

you cannot _____ to look at. One starry night, when the family was ready to move
$\qquad$ 9

away from the farm, Emil stood outside with his father. His father, who was a very silent man, seemed as

though he was about to talk. When he did say something, he surprised Emil by saying that because the

family _____ on a journey to California, _____ for Emil
$\qquad$ 10 $\qquad$ 11

to leave the family and _____. That was the beginning of the journey that led Emil
$\qquad$ 12

to become Father Emil.

5 | *Interpreting the Characters*

Read the following questions and answers. The answers are not mentioned directly in the story, but it is possible to make good guesses based on your knowledge of the story and of American life. Decide whether each answer is *likely* or *unlikely*. Circle your choice. Then, working in small groups, give reasons for your choices and discuss your opinions. There is no one correct answer, but there is more evidence for some choices than for others.

1. Why did Father Emil go to a monastery at the age of eighteen?

   a) He had probably felt attracted to the religious life for   *likely*   *unlikely*
   a long time.

   b) During the Great Depression, there were few other   *likely*   *unlikely*
   career opportunities.

   c) His father had once suggested that he go to a   *likely*   *unlikely*
   monastery.

2. Why does Father Emil take long walks in the evening?

   a) He appreciates nature.   *likely*   *unlikely*

   b) Parents in Lake Wobegon have asked him to make   *likely*   *unlikely*
   sure that there are no children on the streets after
   dark.

   c) He considers it part of his work as a priest to check   *likely*   *unlikely*
   on each child.

6 | *Retelling the Story*

Use these phrases to retell the story in your own words. As you speak, try to include as many details as you can. A different student may want to retell each part.

A satellite TV dish salesman came through Lake Wobegon . . .

This information may help you:

- crimson Cadillac
- Father Emil latched on to
- good reception at the Youth Center
- pay it off
- brochure
- skimmed over a few pages

Father Emil is leery of television . . .
- odd people
- no snow or overcast days
- commercials
- go bananas
- Emil's brother from Dallas
- a TV for the rectory

When Father Emil was eighteen years old . . .
- 1931
- bad luck farming
- sold the farm for a truck
- silent man with empty eyes
- load the furniture
- millions of stars
- make something of himself
- hitchhike to a monastery

Now, when Father Emil walks alone at night . . .
- sweater, black topcoat, cap
- slight limp
- waltz
- stars shining
- bluish television light
- attractive men and women
- names of everyone
- blessing

7 | *Telling Your Own Stories*

1 Find out which classmates have had the following experiences. Ask yes/no questions: for example, "Do you think that television is bad for children?" Try to find one classmate for each statement. When you get a "yes" answer, write that classmate's name in the blank. Do not tell any stories yet. To begin the exercise, stand up and move around the classroom freely.

1. _____ thinks that television is bad for children.
     (name)

2. _____ once received some surprising news from a family member.
     (name)

3. _____ remembers clearly how he or she chose a career.
     (name)

4. _____ has been influenced by someone in the religious professions.
     (name)

2 Look at your list above. If several of you have stories for each experience, one of you should volunteer to be the storyteller. You can tell your stories to the whole class or to small groups. If almost everyone has a story to tell, you might want to work in pairs and exchange stories.

8 Getting into the Language

A Notice the Structure: Present Perfect Tense

> "He **has** always **been** leery of television. It's so strange. He doesn't have one himself. And when he **has looked** at it, everything is so odd."

The present perfect tense has many uses. Two examples are shown here. Each of them refers to an indefinite time in the past. The first sentence refers to a feeling that Father Emil has had over a period of time, and which he still has. The second one refers to an action at an indefinite point in time in the past. It does not say specifically when Father Emil looked at TV, but it suggests that he has seen it at least once. In both examples, the present perfect tense is used to connect the past with the present.

> Although he did not buy a satellite TV dish, Father Emil **has been wondering** about the effect of TV on young people ever since that salesman came through town.

In this sentence, you can see another use of the present perfect tense. This sentence refers to an action over a period of time from a specific point in the past up to the present. It says that Father Emil has had thoughts about TV for a period of time that started when he talked to the satellite TV dish salesman.

> **Present Perfect Tense** *(have/has [not] + past participle)*
>
> SALESMAN: Father, what **have** you **heard** about satellite TV dishes?
>
> **Present Perfect Continuous Tense** *(have/has + been + VERB-ing)*
>
> SALESMAN: Our new 3.5-meter model dish **has been selling** very well here in Minnesota and the Dakotas over the last six months.

In conversation or in writing, the present perfect tense is often used to begin a topic. Then the speaker or writer usually changes to another tense. For example, in the story about Father Emil, the storyteller introduces the topic of TV with the present perfect tense, then changes to the simple present tense to talk about the general characteristics of TV. It is also possible to bring up a topic with the present perfect tense, then to continue by telling a story about a specific past experience, using the simple past tense.

Read the following letter from Father Emil to his brother in Dallas. Notice the italicized verbs. Each one is marked with a letter to indicate one of the following four categories:

A: present perfect continuous tense for an action over a period of time from a specific point in the past up to the present

B: present perfect tense for an action over a period of time from an indefinite time in the past up to the present

C: simple present tense for a habitual action

D: simple past tense for an action at a specific point in the past

My dearest brother,

I want to thank you for your recent visit and your kind offer to buy a television for the rectory. Since you left, I *have been thinking* [A] that my refusal was a little too blunt, and that you deserve an explanation of my feelings.

For many years now, I *have thought* [B] that television *is* [C] a mixed blessing. When you and I *were* [D] children, we *had* [D] no such thing as TV. However, because of TV, today's children *know* [C] so much more about their world than we ever *did* [D] at their age. I also think that TV *has made* [B] it more difficult for families to talk to one another. Television *is* [C] such a strong influence on family life. For example, last week, I *made* [D] a personal visit to a family in our parish, and the whole time I *was* [D] there, the children *had* [D] cartoons on in their bedrooms, and all the while, the parents *kept* [D] interrupting our conversation to check the football scores on TV...

B Practice the Structures

Read the following paragraph and fill in the blanks with the appropriate form of the verbs in parentheses.

Father Emil _____*has been*_____ leery of television for many years. And on many
                        (1. be)

different occasions in the past, he _____ against it in his church on Sunday.
                                            (2. speak)

For example, about fifteen years ago, he _____ against it, and
                                                    (3. preach)

_____ his parishioners sign a promise to turn their TV sets to the wall on
        (4. make)

Saturday and Sunday. He _____ that his system was a success, but he soon
                                    (5. think)

_____ that although a lot of people in Lake Wobegon did turn their sets to
        (6. discover)

the wall, they _____ mirrors on the other side, or they
                        (7. put)

_____ their sets to a wall with a window and
        (8. turn)

_____ outside to watch. He _____ much
        (9. go)   (10. *negative*, say)

about the subject of TV in church since that time. However, since satellite TV became available in Lake

Wobegon, he _____ about it again.
                    (11. think)

9 Extending the Story in Writing

A Writing Down a Story

Write down a story from Exercise 7, either one you heard or your own. If you choose another student's story, show your work to the storyteller when you finish. Ask the storyteller to comment on your version. Then revise the story, making any necessary changes and corrections.

B Writing a Personal Letter

Model

When Father Emil's brother came up from Dallas a few years ago, he offered to buy Emil a TV set for the rectory, but Emil refused, saying, "I would have made a good monk." Several weeks later, Emil wrote a short letter to his brother, explaining in more detail why he did not want a TV. The beginning of his letter appears in Exercise 8. Look at it again and notice how he mentions the personal experience and observations that he has had over a long period of time, using the present perfect tense. Then he gives more detail by telling a specific story about the past, using the past tense, or he makes comments about the general nature of TV, using the present tense.

Assignment

Write a letter to a friend, explaining your thoughts on the subject of TV. You might want to write about the effects that TV has on children or the family. Or you might want to write about the differences that you have noticed between TV in the U.S. and TV in other countries. As you write, try to use the language and the structures from this unit.

UNIT 8
Storm Home

1 Judging from Experience

Read the questions. Discuss the answers with your classmates.

1. Look at the drawing. Why might a child want to go into this cottage?
2. What are some examples of "storms," or problems, in a child's life?
3. Look at the title. What do you think this story is about?

Part One

A Vocabulary

Read the sentences and find the word or expression in the box that means the same as the italicized words. Then compare your answers with those of a classmate. If you disagree, consult another classmate, a dictionary or your teacher.

1. _____ Some teenagers are not very neat. They have clothes and papers *strewn* all over their bedrooms.

2. _____ The girl was so anxious to read the letter from her boyfriend that she *ripped open* the envelope.

3. _____ Farmers spend a lot of time caring for and feeding their *livestock*.

4. _____ The *Holsteins* need to be milked twice a day.

5. _____ When choosing movies for young people, you should avoid *horror shows* because they are often violent and frightening.

6. _____ Most people *figure* that life in the countryside is safer and more peaceful than life in the city.

7. _____ If neither of us is looking for a specific item, let's just *roam* around the shopping center and look at everything.

8. _____ It was the first time the teenager had been caught speeding on the highway, so the police officer gave him a *caution* rather than a ticket.

9. _____ It is a mistake to read in light that is *dim* because you can injure your eyes.

10. _____ At the end of this course, *I'll bet* that there will be an examination of some kind.

11. _____ If you want to get to the center of town, you can *catch* the bus on this corner.

12. _____ In Minnesota, there are severe *blizzards* every winter. Many schools and businesses have to close because of the dangerously cold weather.

a) not bright
b) wander
c) scattered here and there
d) believe, conclude
e) take
f) films that create a feeling of intense fear or terror
g) dairy cows
h) tore apart
i) warning
j) I'm sure
k) animals
l) snowstorms

B Getting the Gist of the Story

In severe climates, school officials sometimes have to make special arrangements to protect the children. In this story, Garrison thinks back to when he was a child living out in the country and had to travel into town to school every day. He remembers the school's plan for winter emergencies.

Listen to Part One of the story. Read the question and write your answer. Then compare your answer with those of your classmates.

What is a storm home?

_____

 # C Listening for Detail

Listen again to Part One. Circle the letter of the statements that answer the question. (One, two, three or all four statements may be true in each case.) Then compare your answers with those of a classmate. Listen again if you disagree with each other.

1. What did Rollie Hochstetter do last Tuesday?

  a) He went into town.

  b) He bought a belt for his wood saw.

  c) He stayed away from the farm for more than half the day.

  d) He butchered some ducks and geese.

2. Rollie figured that wild dogs had been at the farm. Why?

  a) The cows were very frightened.

  b) There were dog tracks in the snow.

  c) Dead dogs were lying nearby.

  d) Some people had seen wild dogs recently.

3. Why were the younger children so scared of the wild dogs?

  a) They had seen the dogs.

  b) The school is near Rollie's farm.

  c) The children walked to school through the dark woods.

  d) They believed that the dogs were hungry.

4. What was different for Garrison when he started seventh grade?

  a) He entered high school.

  b) He did not walk to school anymore.

  c) He lived in town.

  d) He was no longer assigned to a storm home.

Part Two

$\boxed{D}$ Vocabulary

Read the sentences and find the word or expression in the box that means the same as the italicized words. Then compare your answers with those of a classmate. If you disagree, consult another classmate, a dictionary or your teacher.

1. _____ When I was cleaning out my desk, I *came across* some old pictures.

2. _____ We had to climb up a tall tree in order to *rescue* our cat.

3. _____ After a meal, I often *feel like* eating something sweet.

4. _____ After being outdoors on a cold day, it is nice to warm up with a cup of hot *chocolate*.

5. _____ *Oatmeal* cookies with raisins make a healthy snack.

6. _____ We were talking about her, and then she suddenly was there *in the flesh, big as life.*

7. _____ All of my troubles were *bearable* because my friends were able to help me.

a) physically present

b) made from whole grain oat

c) milk and cocoa

d) found

e) save

f) acceptable

g) want to

$\boxed{E}$ Predicting and Listening 📼

1 Working in small groups. discuss the question. Predict what might happen next in the story. Write down at least two possible answers.

Did Garrison ever visit his storm home? Why or why not?

a. _____

b. _____

c. _____

2 Keeping your same groups, listen to the end of the story. Discuss how your predictions were different from the ending you heard.

F Listening for Detail

Listen again to Part Two. Circle the letters of the statements that answer the question. (One, two, three or all four statements may be true in each case.) Then compare your answers with those of a classmate. Listen again if you disagree with each other.

1. Which statements describe the Kruegers' home?

   a) It was in town.

   b) It was small and green.

   c) It was a cottage near the lake.

   d) The house was neat and delicate.

2. What situations did Garrison imagine?

   a) He imagined disliking the Kruegers.

   b) He imagined going to live with the Kruegers forever.

   c) He imagined himself in a story.

   d) He imagined meeting the Kruegers.

3. Garrison dreamed of visiting the Kruegers. In his imagination, what would Mrs. Krueger do?

   a) She would invite him in and offer him dry clothes.

   b) She would offer him something to eat and drink.

   c) She would call his parents.

   d) She would play cards with him.

4. Why didn't Garrison ever meet the Kruegers?

   a) He did not have any problems at all.

   b) There were no blizzards during school hours.

   c) He was later assigned to a different storm home.

   d) The Kruegers did not want a storm child.

3 Getting the Joke

Read each item and decide which answer explains why the audience laughs. Circle your choice. Then, working in groups, compare your answers. If you agree, discuss the reasons for your choices. If you disagree, discuss your opinions and try to come to an agreement. In each case, there is one choice that best explains the joke.

1. "When they got back home, they found about sixteen chickens and ducks and geese strewn out down the snow, . . . all bloody in the snow. And all the other livestock [was] upset, even the Holsteins, who looked like they'd been to a horror show and wanted to jump over the fence and into somebody's arms."
The cows were so frightened by what they saw that they

   a) looked like they were in a movie.

   b) turned pale.

   c) seemed almost human.

2. "And Mrs. Krueger would open the door, and she'd say, 'Oh! It's you. I knew you'd come someday. I'm so glad to see you.'"
Garrison could imagine Mrs. Krueger's exact words because he

   a) had other, similar friends.

   b) had thought about visiting her so many times.

   c) knew other children who had had the Kruegers as a storm home.

3. "She'd say, 'Carl, come on down here. See what's in the kitchen!' He'd say, 'Is it our storm child?' She'd say, 'Yes! He's sitting here in the flesh, big as life!'"
In his imagination, Garrison was so important to the Kruegers that, when he finally arrived at their home, they would

   a) welcome him as a long-awaited guest.

   b) not believe he was real.

   c) want him to stay forever.

4. "We didn't have any blizzards that came during the day that year or the year after that. They were all convenient blizzards— evening, weekend blizzards."
The idea of a "convenient blizzard" is humorous because it is

   a) a childish notion.

   b) very scientific.

   c) a complete contradiction.

4 Reviewing Vocabulary

Fill in each blank with one of these words or expressions. Be sure to use the correct form of the italicized words. Then compare your answers with those of a classmate.

rip open   *figure*   *roam*   *rescue*
blizzard   *strew*   dim   *come* across
bearable   *feel* like   livestock

On Tuesday, a number of chickens, geese and ducks were killed at the Hochstetters' farm. When they returned from town, the property was _____ 1 with dead birds. The Hochstetters _____ 2 several that had had their throats _____ 3. They _____ 4 that wild dogs had done it, since neighbors had seen some dogs _____ 5 around in the woods. The Holsteins and other _____ 6 were frightened by the bloody scene, and so were the children who had to walk through the woods to school in the _____ 7 morning and late afternoon light. It was especially scary because the older children told the younger ones that the dogs were nearby, looking for their next meal.

Another frightening thing about growing up in Lake Wobegon was the possibility of being lost in a _____ 8. So each Lake Wobegon schoolchild who lived far from town was assigned to a "storm home" near the school. Garrison's storm home was the Kruegers'. They owned a small, green cottage down by the lake. He often _____ 9 knocking on the door. He always imagined that the kindly Kruegers _____ 10 him from life's problems if he needed help.

Although he never actually went to his storm home, it seemed to Garrison that life's problems were more _____ 11 because he could imagine going there whenever things got difficult.

Read the following questions and answers. The answers are not mentioned directly in the story, but it is possible to make good guesses based on your knowledge of the story and of American life. Decide whether each answer is *likely* or *unlikely*. Circle your choice. Then, working in small groups, give reasons for your choices and discuss your opinions. There is no one correct answer, but there is more evidence for some choices than for others.

1. Why did the older children of Lake Wobegon like to scare the younger ones with stories about hungry wild dogs in the woods?

   a) The older children really wanted to be mean and scare them.   *likely   unlikely*

   b) By scaring the younger children, the older ones got rid of some of their own fear.   *likely   unlikely*

   c) Their parents had told them the same stories.   *likely   unlikely*

2. Whenever he had troubles, why did Garrison think, "Well, there's always the Kruegers"?

   a) He figured the Kruegers would be able to help him with almost any problem he had because they were older and more sympathetic than his own parents.   *likely   unlikely*

   b) As a child, he was often scared and unhappy at home and needed a place to escape to.   *likely   unlikely*

   c) The idea of havnig a safe place to go, even though he never really went, helped him deal with his problems.   *likely   unlikely*

| 6 | *Retelling the Story* |

Use these phrases to retell the story in your own words. As you speak, try to include as many details as you can. A different student may want to retell each part.

Rollie Hochstetter needed a new belt for his woodsaw . . .

This information may help you:

- went into town
- two or three hours
- chickens, ducks, geese
- horror show
- wild dogs roaming
- walk through the woods
- older children scare younger ones

When he went into the seventh grade,
Garrison caught the bus . . .

- Lake Wobegon High
  School in town
- "Your storm home is . . ."
- the Kruegers
- neat, green cottage
- kindly old couple

He imagined going to his storm home . . .

- knock on the Kruegers'
  door
- oatmeal cookies and
  chocolate
- "Is it our storm child?"
- in the flesh, big as life
- only convenient blizzards
- whenever things got difficult

7 Telling Your Own Stories

1 Find out which classmates have had the following experiences. Ask yes/no
questions: for example, "Have you been in a scary situation because of bad
weather?" Try to find one classmate for each statement. When you get a "yes"
answer, write that classmate's name in the blank. Do not tell any stories yet. To
begin the exercise, stand up and move around the room freely.

1. _____ has been in a scary situation because of bad weather.
   (name)

2. _____ remembers a story that older children used to tell in order
   (name)   to scare younger children.

3. _____ has been able to talk more easily with someone outside
   (name)   the family.

4. _____ had or still has a "storm home" when things get difficult.
   (name)

2 Look at your list above. If several of you have stories for each experience, one
of you should volunteer to be the storyteller. You can tell your stories to the
whole class or to small groups. If almost everyone has a story to tell, you
might want to work in pairs and exchange stories.

8 | *Getting into the Language*

A | *Notice the Structure: Present Unreal Conditions*

> If you **were** a child lost in a dark forest, you **would know** there was a kindly old couple living in this cottage.

Use the present unreal pattern for a situation that is impossible or unreal. Notice that, in this construction, the past form of the verb does not refer to past time. Instead, it refers to a present or future situation that is not possible or real. When the *if* clause begins a sentence, put a comma after it. No comma is needed when the *if* clause ends a sentence. Also notice that *were* is the only correct form of the verb *be* in the *if* clause.

Present Unreal Conditions

If + past form , *would (not)* + base form.
                            could
                            might

would + base form (logical result)	If Lake Wobegon **allowed** it, Rollie **would shoot** the dogs on sight. (Lake Wobegon does not allow it.)
	If I **were** Rollie Hochstetter, I **would not take** any chances. I **would build** a stronger fence around my chickens and geese. (I am not Rollie Hochstetter.)
could + base form (possibility)	Rollie isn't sure what he is going to do. He **could reinforce** the fence he has now, or he **could purchase** an electric fence if he **decided** to invest more money. (He has not decided to invest more money.)
might + base form (weak possibility)	The Mayor of Lake Wobegon doesn't like to spend money, and so far Rollie is the only person complaining about the wild dogs. But, if other farmers **had** trouble with them, Rollie **might be able** to get some help to deal with the problem. (Other farmers have not had trouble with the dogs.)

B Practice the Structure

1 Rewrite each sentence as an unreal condition. Notice that the *if* clause will come at the beginning of some sentences but at the end of others. You may have to make other small changes in the sentences.

a. Because children are scared of the dark, they have nightmares.

If children were not scared of the dark, they would not have nightmares.

b. Because all of us have troubles, we need storm homes.

c. Some children in Lake Wobegon look forward to blizzards because they have storm homes to go to. (Use *might*.)

d. Because the Kruegers live in town, they are eligible to be "storm parents." (Use *could*.)

e. Mrs. Krueger always signs up for the storm home program partly because she doesn't have any children of her own. (Use *might*.)

f. Because she does not like packaged oatmeal cookies, Mrs. Kreuger does not buy them.

2 Imagine yourself as the person indicated. Write an unreal conditional sentence about it. Begin your sentence with: *If I were . . .*

a. Mrs. Krueger *If I were Mrs. Krueger, I would want Garrison to visit me.*

b. Garrison Keillor _____

_____

c. a student at Lake Wobegon High School _____

_____

d. Mr. Dettman, the principal _____

_____

e. a parent whose children travel a long distance to school _____

_____

f. a weather forecaster in Minnesota _____

_____

9 Extending the Story in Writing

A Writing Down a Story

Write down a story from Exercise 7, either one you heard or your own. If you choose another person's story, show your work to the storyteller when you finish. Ask the storyteller to comment on your version. Then revise the story, making any necessary changes and corrections.

B Writing a Business Letter

A business letter is usually a request for information, attention or action. While you may or may not know the person to whom you are writing, you need not make the letter too formal. In fact, a direct and simple style is best.

In the first paragraph, establish your relationship with the reader: *As a long-time customer, I regret . . .* ; or *I recently read your advertisement in . . .* ; or *Since you already know the value of up-to-date information, you may be interested in . . . .* Use the middle paragraph to discuss your main purpose and the final paragraph to make your request specific: *I hope to hear from you soon*; or *Please send in your order on the enclosed form*; or *I look forward to receiving the information soon.*

Model

Here is part of a recent business letter that Mr. Dettman, the principal of Lake Wobegon High School, wrote to ask nearby residents to sign up for the storm home program. It is an example of a "form letter," since copies of the same letter were sent to all eligible residents; only the names and addresses changed.

=== **Lake Wobegon High School** ===
Lake Wobegon, Minnesota 55112

September 10, 1990

Mr. and Mrs. Leland Krueger
20 Lakeside Drive
Lake Wobegon, MN 55112

Dear Mr. and Mrs. Krueger,

   As you know, for many years neighborhood residents have taken pride in participating in Lake Wobegon High School activities. If you were a child from the countryside, you would know just how important the storm home program has been in the past. I am writing to ask your continued assistance with this necessary service.
   If you volunteer to participate, one student will be assigned to you . . . .

He closed his letter in this way:

Sincerely yours,

William Dettman,
Principal

Assignment

Complete Mr. Dettman's letter. He will inform town residents about the need for a storm home program, tell town residents how they would be notified if there were a blizzard, tell them what they should do, and request that they indicate their acceptance in writing. Follow the business letter format as shown, and try to use the vocabulary and structures from the unit.

Here is some advice on writing an effective business letter from Malcolm Forbes, president and editor-in-chief of *Forbes,* a major American business magazine:

Write the entire letter from his [or her] point of view — what's in it for him? Beat him to the draw: surprise him by answering the questions and objections he might have. . . .

Be natural — *write the way you talk.* Imagine him sitting in front of you. What would you say to him? . . .

The acid test: Read your letter out loud when you're done.

UNIT 9
Starting the Car in Winter

1 *Judging from Experience*

Read the questions. Discuss the answers with your classmates.

1. Look at the drawing. Why do you suppose these cars have their hoods up and
   their engines connected by jumper cables?
2. How do you use jumper cables?

2 Listening

Part One

A Vocabulary

1 Read the sentences and find the word or expression in the box that means the same as the italicized words. Then compare your answers with those of a classmate. If you disagree, consult another classmate, a dictionary or your teacher.

1. _____ One of the best cars ever made was the 1953 *Chevy*.

2. _____ To start a car, *pump* the gas pedal several times. Then turn the key.

3. _____ If you keep the gas pedal down too far, when you start a car, the engine makes a big *roar*.

4. _____ Many car repair people are *trustworthy*; they do a good job at a fair price.

5. _____ If your car is in a bad accident, *there is no point* in trying to repair it.

6. _____ In the equation d = r ÷ t, the three *variables* are distance, rate and time.

7. _____ When your car does not start, sometimes all that you have to do is *fiddle with* the engine.

8. _____ If the *carburetor* is dirty, your car will not run well.

9. _____ It can be *maddening* to try to fix a car because there are so many things that could possibly be wrong.

10. _____ Minnesota's winter temperatures can get down to *thirty-some below*.

11. _____ Most of us feel that *transplants* are medical miracles: it is difficult to understand how a part of one person's body can be used to keep another person alive.

12. _____ The human body is made of many different *tissues*—bone, muscle, nerve and so on.

13. _____ On a cold winter day, you can wear a heavy *parka* to keep out the wind and the cold.

a) dependable

b) push up and down with the foot

c) very annoying

d) loud, deep sound

e) move or touch, with no clear purpose

f) about −30° F

g) things that can change in size or quantity

h) short coat with a protective cover for the head, often made with fur

i) things that are moved from one place to another

j) device in an engine that mixes gasoline with air

k) cells of a living thing, especially those alike in form or purpose

l) there is no purpose

m) Chevrolet: a brand of American automobile

2 Circle the letter of the expression that is closest in meaning to the italicized word or phrase. Then compare your answers with those of a classmate.

1. Winters in Minnesota can be *bitterly* cold and very long.

   a) acidly   **b)** extremely   **c)** moderately

2. The cold and dark winters in Minnesota *depress* some of the people who live there.

   a) sadden   **b)** excite   **c)** freeze

3. The long Minnesota winters can *be hard to take.*

   a) be difficult to understand   **b)** be difficult to avoid

   c) be difficult to tolerate

4. The heart-transplant patient died after two weeks. The doctors were not sure why the new heart did not *take.*

   a) grow   **b)** survive   **c)** move

5. Sometimes it is difficult to stay *cool* when you are working under pressure.

   a) interested   **b)** excited   **c)** calm

6. It is getting *chilly* in here; please close the windows.

   a) cool   **b)** dark   **c)** smoky

7. One way to make coffee is to use a special pot: you put water in the bottom and ground beans in a metal basket on the top. After about five or ten minutes on the stove, the coffee begins to *perk.*

   a) burn in the pot   **b)** pour out of the pot

   c) boil up and drip down in the pot

B | *Getting the Gist of the Story*

In this story, Lyle Janske and his brother-in-law, Carl Krepsbach, learn something about how to ask for help and how to accept it.

Listen to Part One of the story. Read the questions and write your answers. Then compare your answers with those of a classmate.

1. What is Carl Krepsbach proud of?

_____

_____

2. What does Lyle Janske worry about?

_____

_____

C Listening for Detail

Listen again to Part One. Circle the letter of the answer that best completes each sentence. Then compare your answers with those of a classmate. Listen again if you disagree with each other.

1. Lyle Janske, Carl's brother-in-law, lives next door. When he hears Carl's car start right up in the morning, he

   a) wonders what is wrong.

   b) is happy for Carl.

   c) feels depressed.

2. Carl sometimes comes over to Lyle's house to

   a) borrow Lyle's jumper cables.

   b) start Lyle's car.

   c) cheer Lyle up.

3. Lyle has trouble with winter weather because he is from

   a) Minnesota.

   b) California.

   c) South Carolina.

4. When Lyle went to take a shower on Monday morning, it did not make him feel better because

   a) there was no water.

   b) the water was too hot.

   c) the water was too cold.

5. While Lyle was making his morning coffee, he heard

   a) Carl come into the house.

   b) Carl's coffee perking.

   c) Carl's car engine.

Part Two

D Vocabulary

Read the sentences and find the word or expression in the box that means the same as the italicized words. Then compare your answers with those of a classmate. If you disagree, consult another classmate, a dictionary or your teacher.

1. _____ A very sick person may not be able to speak. He or she may only *moan*.

2. _____ You can burn *charcoal* for heat. If you are an artist, you can use small sticks of it for drawing.

3. _____ When a car gets stuck in the snow, sometimes the passengers have to get out and *shove* it.

4. _____ If your car gets stuck very badly, you can use a big truck and a heavy chain to *haul* it out.

5. _____ If you leave a cigarette in an ashtray, it will *smolder* for about twenty minutes.

6. _____ Rotten eggs and dead fish make a *stench*.

7. _____ Cooking oil is *combustible*, so you must not allow it to get too hot.

8. _____ If you want to heat some water, putting the *lid* on the pot will make it boil sooner.

9. _____ Sometimes the *coals* left after a forest fire continue to burn for weeks.

10. _____ Sometimes children are not very careful: they come *barreling* up the sidewalk on their bicycles.

a) burn slowly

b) top

c) make a low cry

d) easily burned

e) terrible smell

f) push

g) small pieces of burning wood

h) traveling fast

i) pull

j) black substance made of partially burned wood

E Predicting and Listening

1 Working in small groups, discuss the question. Predict what might happen next in the story. Write down at least two possible answers.

What will Lyle Janske do to try to start his car?

a. _____

_____

b. _____

_____

c. _____

_____

2 Keeping your same groups, listen to the end of the story. Discuss how your predictions were different from the ending you heard.

$\boxed{F}$ *Listening for Detail* 📼

Listen again to Part Two. Circle the letter of the answer that best completes each sentence. Then compare your answers with those of a classmate. Listen again if you disagree with each other.

1. Lyle was desperate to get his car started because he did not want

  a) to be late for work.

  b) Carl to help him.

  c) to have to call the repair garage.

2. Lyle made a fire in the garbage can lid because he wanted to

  a) burn the garbage.

  b) warm up his hands.

  c) heat up the car engine.

3. When the fire department truck came barreling up to Lyle's garage,

  a) the firefighters called Carl.

  b) Lyle told the firefighters to leave.

  c) everybody in the neighborhood came over.

4. When the neighbors asked how it happened, the firefighters did not answer because

  a) they did not know the cause of the fire.

  b) it was too embarrassing.

  c) Lyle told them not to.

5. After the fire was out, Carl

  a) tried to comfort Lyle.

  b) drove Lyle to work.

  c) began to work on Lyle's car.

3 Getting the Joke

Read each item and decide which answer explains why the audience laughs. Circle your choice. Then, working in groups, compare your answers. If you agree, discuss the reasons for your choices. If you disagree, discuss your opinions and try to come to an agreement. In each case, there is one choice that best explains the joke.

1. "And Lyle's car is an old Chevy, too, which leaves just one variable in the equation, and that's Lyle."
Carl can always start his car, but Lyle cannot start his because of

   a) human error.

   b) mechanical trouble.

   c) bad luck.

2. "Even on bitterly, bitterly cold mornings, Carl goes out to his garage, and he gets in his old Chevy, and he pumps the gas pedal about eight or ten times. . . . She jumps right up. Starts right up. . . . And sometimes Carl doesn't even need to use jumper cables!"
Using jumper cables in Minnesota in the winter is often the only way to start a car. For Lyle, the fact that Carl does not always need to use jumper cables is

   a) reassuring

   b) incomprehensible.

   c) exciting.

3. "Lyle was born, and grew up, and spent most of his life in Southern California. He's lived in Lake Wobegon now for almost ten years, but some of these transplants don't take, you know. Some of these Southerners who move up to the North, their tissues reject winter."
Lyle's move from California to Minnesota has been like an unsuccessful

   a) vacation.

   b) career.

   c) organ transplant.

4. "Even his wife felt chilly to him. She's from Minnesota. Lyle kind of thinks that her temperature drops during the winter, like bears."
Lyle compares his wife to a bear because she

   a) is not bothered by the cold.

   b) is difficult to awaken.

   c) gets as angry as a bear does.

5. "Carl is also the captain of the volunteer fire department. He was the one who made the call. He was also the first one on the scene."
It is humorous that Carl is also a member of the town's non-professional fire-fighting team because

   a) the fire was right next door.

   b) Carl's house could have caught on fire, too.

   c) the fire gave Carl another opportunity to help Lyle.

6. "Carl put his arm around Lyle, and he smiled at him, and he said, 'You should have called me up. I would have come over and helped you! What are brothers-in-law for?' "
Carl smiled at Lyle and put his arm around him because he wanted Lyle to

   a) forget about it

   b) ask for help the next time.

   c) feel worse than he already did.

4 Reviewing Vocabulary

Fill in each blank with one of these words or expressions. Be sure to use the correct form of the italicized words. Compare your answers with those of a classmate.

combustible	maddening	*haul*
bitter	*shove*	*depress*
stench	moan	parka
lid	*smolder*	*be* hard to take
there *be* no point in	transplant	coals

Winter in Minnesota is often _____ cold. When the temperature goes down to
                                              1
−30° Fahrenheit and below, it is hard for people to start their cars. This is especially true for Lyle Janske,

in Lake Wobegon. He has an old Chevy, and when it is that cold, _____ trying to
                                                                                              2
start it. It is just impossible. However, Lyle's brother-in-law, Carl, does not ever have any trouble starting

his own Chevy.

Lyle is a _____ to Minnesota from Southern California, and he truly dislikes
                              3
winter. What really _____ Lyle, however, is the fact that Carl can be so helpful.
                                  4
He comes over to Lyle's house in his big winter _____ and boots and he starts
                                                                  5
Lyle's car for him with absolutely no trouble, which Lyle finds _____. He thinks
                                                                                  6
Carl's helpfulness _____ rather _____.
                                                                      7

One morning recently, Lyle tried to start his car, but the only sound it made was a long

_____. Lyle decided he would absolutely not accept Carl's help again, so he made
              8
a charcoal fire in the garbage can _____ and got some hot
                                                          9
_____ burning. Then he _____ it under the engine and
              10   11
went back inside the house. Within minutes, the car _____, producing a great deal
                                                                            12
of smoke and a terrible _____ that everybody in town could smell. When the
                                          13
firefighters came, they _____ the smoking car out and saved the garage. Lyle was
                                      14
surprised by the whole incident, since he had not realized that his car would still be

_____ at thirty-some degrees below zero.
              15

5 Interpreting the Characters

Read the following questions and answers. The answers are not mentioned directly in the story, but it is possible to make good guesses based on your knowledge of the story and of American life. Decide whether each answer is *likely* or *unlikely*. Circle your choice. Then, working in small groups, give reasons for your choices and discuss your opinions. There is no one correct answer, but there is more evidence for some choices than for others.

1. Why is Lyle so annoyed by Carl?

   a) Carl usually can solve problems that Lyle cannot solve.   *likely*   *unlikely*

   b) Carl probably makes jokes about him to try to embarrass him.   *likely*   *unlikely*

   c) Lyle prefers not to accept help from his wife's family.   *likely*   *unlikely*

2. Why did Lyle put a garbage can lid of hot coals under his car's engine?

   a) He wanted to prove his ability to Carl.   *likely*   *unlikely*

   b) He wanted to save money and not buy an electric heater like those that other Minnesotans use to warm their car engines.   *likely*   *unlikely*

   c) He did it as a scientific experiment.   *likely*   *unlikely*

6 Retelling the Story

Use these phrases to retell the story in your own words. As you speak, try to include as many details as you can. A different student may want to retell each part.

People in Lake Wobegon are proud of having cars that start in the coldest weather . . .

This information may help you:

- Carl Krepsbach
- forty-five degrees below zero
- Lyle Janske, Carl's brother-in-law
- the roar of Carl's engine
- depressing
- not trustworthy
- no point in trying
- jumper cables
- fiddle with something
- hard to take

Lyle is the science teacher at the high school . . .

- can explain cold
- Southern California
- transplants
- "Cool Carl" in his parka

Lyle woke up on Monday morning . . .

- wife chilly
- like bears
- shower
- made coffee
- heard roar
- Lyle was desperate
- charcoal in a garbage can lid
- shoved

Carl is the captain of the volunteer fire department . . . .

- everybody came
- smoldered
- stench
- hard to explain the fire
- "That man is teaching our children about science!"
- combustible
- saved the garage
- Carl put his arm around Lyle
- brothers-in-law

7 | *Telling Your Own Stories*

1 Find out which classmates have had the following experiences. Ask yes/no questions: for example, "Have you ever had problems adjusting to a different climate?" Try to find one classmate for each statement. When you get a "yes" answer, write that classmate's name in the blank. Do not tell any stories yet. To begin the exercise, stand up and move around the classroom freely.

1. _____ has had problems adjusting to a different climate.
      (name)

2. _____ has felt frustrated by a machine that did not work.
      (name)

3. _____ has helped someone solve a problem.
      (name)

4. _____ has refused someone's help when he or she should have
      (name)   accepted it.

2 Look at your list above. If several of you have stories for each experience, one of you should volunteer to be the storyteller. You can tell your stories to the whole class or to small groups. If almost everyone has a story to tell, you might want to work in pairs and exchange stories.

 Getting into the Language

 Notice the Structures: Modal Perfects and Past Unreal Conditionals

> After the fire, Carl put his arm around Lyle's shoulder, smiled at him and said, "You **should have called** me up. **I would have come** over and **helped** you."

Modal perfects, which are forms of modal auxiliary verbs, are used with past participles to refer to situations in the past. Although there are many such modals, in this exercise you see just two of these forms: *should (not) have* and *would (not) have*. The other structures in this exercise are past unreal conditions, in which *if* is used to talk about past situations that are contrary to what actually happened.

***should (not) have* + past participle** Refers to a past action that was a good idea but did not happen. It can also refer to a regret about the past.	I **should have gotten** a used car. (Getting a used car was a good idea, but I did not do it.) I **should not have bought** a new car. (I bought a new car, but I regret it.)
***If* + *had (not)* + past participle . . . *would (not) have* + past participle** Refer to past situations that are contrary to what actually happened.	I told my sister about the bill for the repairs on my new car, and she said, "**If** you **had asked** me, I **would have helped** you find a good used car, and you **would not have wasted** your money." (I did not ask her for help, so she did not help me and I wasted my money.)

Note that sometimes it is possible to use *would (not) have* + past participle without an *if* clause. However, there is an unspoken, implied *if* statement. Look at this example:

"Carl put his arm around Lyle's shoulder, smiled at him and said, 'You **should have called** me up. I **would have come** over and **helped** you.'" (Carl did not come over and help Lyle start his car. Instead of using the modal phrase *should have called,* Carl also could have used an *if* clause: "**If you had called me up,** I **would have come** over and **helped** you.")

B | Practice the Structure

1 About two weeks after the fire, Lyle Janske was still thinking about the fire. Here are some of his thoughts. Fill in each blank with the correct modal perfect form of *should* and the verb in parentheses.

"After the fire, Carl told me that I ___*should have called*___ him. Actually, I'm still trying
(1. call)

to figure out how the fire happened. Perhaps I _____ less charcoal in the
(2. put)

garbage can lid. The fire I made was too hot. But I didn't use that much. Maybe I went in the house too

soon. I imagine that I _____ inside to warm up. I wasn't able to watch the
(3. *negative*, go)

coals closely. It was so cold outside, though! I just had to go back in and get a cup of coffee. However, I

_____ only one cup of coffee, not two. The fire had a chance to spread.
(4. drink)

That coffee smelled so good, though. I guess that's why I didn't smell the smoke from the garage. I

_____ the stench coming from the fire earlier. The firefighters arrived
(5. notice)

before I could even read the directions on the fire extinguisher that Carl gave me for my birthday. When

they saw the garbage can lid full of hot coals, I felt so stupid. Fortunately, the whole thing was over in only

twenty minutes. However, I _____ the coffee pot on the stove while the
(6. *negative*, leave)

fire department was here. I burned the pot and Carl offered me a new one so cheerfully. I think I'd rather

drink tea."

2 Look at these sentences. Rewrite each pair as one sentence, using a past unreal conditional.

   a. Carl told me that I should have called him up. He didn't come over to help me start the car.

Carl told me that if I had called him up,
he would have come over to help me start the car.

   b. Perhaps I should have put less charcoal in the garbage can lid. The fire I made was too hot.

_____

_____

   c. I imagine that I shouldn't have gone inside to warm up. I wasn't able to watch the coals closely.

_____

_____

   d. However, I should have drunk only one cup of coffee, not two. The fire had a chance to spread.

_____

_____

   e. I should have noticed the stench coming from the fire earlier. I didn't have a chance to call the fire department myself.

_____

_____

   f. I shouldn't have left the coffee pot on the stove while the fire department was here. I burned the pot and Carl offered me a new one so cheerfully.

_____

_____

9   *Extending the Story in Writing*

A   *Writing Down a Story*

Write down a story from Exercise 7, either one you heard or your own. If you choose another student's story, show your work to the storyteller when you finish. Ask the storyteller to comment on your version. Then revise the story, making any necessary changes and corrections.

B Writing a Personal Letter: Two Points of View

Read this news item, which appeared in the *Lake Wobegon Herald-Star* following the fire in Lyle's garage.

Local Garage Fire

A smoky fire broke out early Monday morning in the garage of Lyle Janske. Janske's neighbor and brother-in-law, Carl Krepsbach, turned in the alarm shortly after 8:00 A.M. Krepsbach, captain of the Lake Wobegon Volunteer Fire Department, was first on the scene of the blaze, which was quickly brought under control. Krepsbach, a native Lake Wobegon man, led the fire crew in saving the garage. Janske's automobile, however, suffered considerable damage. Janske, a ten-year Lake Wobegonian originally from Southern California, expressed surprise at the incident. Curious neighbors quickly returned to their homes, since the mercury had dropped below -30°F that morning.

Notice that the tone of this news item is objective; that is, the writer tries simply to state the facts of the incident. Nothing about Lyle's desperation or Carl's cheerfulness is mentioned.

Lyle's personal account of this incident would surely not be the same as Carl's. Neither one is likely to be as objective as the story in the newspaper. Both Lyle and Carl are likely to write about the same event with strong but different feelings. To express his point of view, each would use language to create a special tone. Here are some of the ways in which they might do this:

	Lyle might write:	Carl might write:
adjectives	a *minor* fire	a *dangerous* fire
adverbs	*annoyingly* helpful	*unbelievably* ignorant
modals	*should have stayed* in bed	*could have called* me
conditionals	If I *had known* that	If I *hadn't noticed*

Assignment

Write a letter. Imagine that Carl and Lyle both have cut the news item out of the paper and are sending it along with a letter to a relative. In these letters, they give the "true story" of what happened. Using the basic facts of the story, choose one of the situations below. Remember to use adjectives, adverbs and the language you have studied in this unit. For help with the form of a personal letter, look again at Mrs. Temby's letter in Exercise 9 in Unit 1.

a) Lyle Janske is sitting down on a cold, snowy evening a few weeks after the fire, and he is writing a letter to his sister in Los Angeles, California. He is writing about the car fire, and especially about his feelings toward his brother-in-law, Carl Krepsbach. Write his letter.

b) Carl Krepsbach is sitting down on the same evening to write to his brother, who lives up in International Falls, Minnesota. This town is on the Canadian border, and is one of the coldest towns in the United States. He tells his brother about the car fire and about his feelings toward his brother-in-law, Lyle. Write his letter.

UNIT 10
Ella Anderson's Sunset Years

1 | Judging from Experience

Read the questions. Discuss the answers with your classmates.

1. Look at the drawing. What do you suppose the woman's sign says?
2. Look at the title. What is this story about?

2 Listening

Part One

A Vocabulary

Read the sentences and find the word or expression in the box that means the same as the italicized words. Then compare your answers with those of a classmate. If you disagree, consult another classmate, a dictionary or your teacher.

1. _____ In the spring, many people like to plant flowers outside their homes in carefully arranged flower *beds*.

2. _____ Sailors use many instruments to help them *navigate* safely on the ocean.

3. _____ When you sit in a chair for too long, your legs sometimes *fall asleep*.

4. _____ After *being cooped up* all winter, people in Minnesota are anxious to get outdoors in the spring.

5. _____ Older people often have trouble walking because their muscles and joints become *stiff*.

6. _____ Before the schedule of professional baseball games begins, each team meets for several weeks of *spring training*.

7. _____ Some people are difficult to travel with. They are *bad company* because they complain about everything and ruin the trip for others.

8. _____ When a discussion is highly technical, one's mind has to be *sharp* in order to follow it.

9. _____ If we do the exercises *out of order*, you might not understand the story as well.

10. _____ It is necessary to read recipes carefully. When making a cake, if you *skip* a step, the cake may not rise.

11. _____ Parents must have *faith* that their children will make wise decisions when they grow up and leave home.

a) belief, trust

b) in the wrong sequence

c) being closed inside

d) gardens

e) find their way

f) painful when moved

g) quick and sensitive

h) leave out

i) annoying companions

j) pre-season practice

k) lose feeling or muscle control because of poor blood circulation

B Getting the Gist of the Story

This is a story about Ella and Henry Anderson, an elderly couple, and their grown daughter, Charlotte, and how each of them copes with growing older.

Listen to Part One of the story. Read the question and write your answer. Then compare your answer with those of your classmates.

Ella is lonely. Her husband, Henry, is not such bad company, but he needs Ella's help. What does she do for him?

C Listening for Detail

Listen again to Part One. Circle the letter of the answer that best completes each sentence. Then compare your answers with those of a classmate. Listen again if you disagree with each other.

1. Ella has not been outdoors since Thanksgiving, which is a holiday in late November, because of

    a) her flower bed.

    b) the weather.

    c) her husband.

2. Ella moves slowly around her flower beds because she is

    a) bored.

    b) cold.

    c) old.

3. When Henry takes a train trip on the *Burlington Zephyr,* he does not

    a) leave the house.

    b) say a word.

    c) know where he is going.

4. On Henry's train trip, Fountain City is

    a) the last stop.

    b) the stop before Pepin.

    c) the stop after Pepin.

5. Charlotte, Henry and Ella's daughter, cannot give Henry a train trip because she

    a) has not learned the steps.

    b) does not visit very often.

    c) would get too upset.

Part Two

D | Vocabulary

Read the sentences and find the word or expression in the box that means the same as the italicized words. Then compare your answers with those of a classmate. If you disagree, consult another classmate, a dictionary or your teacher.

1. _____ My hospital bill was very high. I *had a fit* when I saw it.

2. _____ If you arrive at a formal party in jeans, you will *look like a fool.*

3. _____ Some people cannot accept criticism. They *take everything too personally.*

4. _____ Some people get *worried sick* about small problems.

5. _____ A general doctor can take care of your basic needs, but a *specialist* can help you with unusual illnesses.

6. _____ When a patient can describe his or her *symptoms,* the doctor can usually determine what is wrong.

7. _____ Some health problems are *fairly* normal. Everybody has a few aches and pains.

8. _____ Many people would prefer to *go* in their sleep.

a) die
b) signs or indications of sickness
c) are very sensitive in a selfish way
d) became very angry
e) reasonably, rather
f) medical expert
g) appear ridiculous or stupid
h) excessively concerned

E | Predicting and Listening

1 Working in small groups. discuss the question. Predict what might happen next in the story. Write down at least two possible answers.

Neither Henry nor Charlotte is very good company, so Ella tries to relieve her loneliness in other ways. What do you think she does?

a. _____

b. _____

c. _____

2 Keeping your same groups, listen to the end of the story. Discuss how your predictions were different from the ending you heard.

F Listening for Detail

Listen again to Part Two. Circle the letter of the answer that best completes each sentence. Then compare your answers with those of a classmate. Listen again if you disagree with each other.

1. The story takes place in

   a) Wisconsin.

   b) 1917.

   c) 1984.

2. What did the sign Ella put into her flower bed look like?

a)

> *Visitors Welcome*
> *Free Coffee*
> *Come In*

c)

> *Visitors Welcome*
> *Free Coffee*
> *Come In*

b)

> Visitors Welcome
> Free Coffee
> Come In

3. Charlotte heard about her mother's sign from

   a) Ella herself.

   b) Henry.

   c) the neighbors.

4. Besides her health, Charlotte worries most about

   a) her parents.

   b) what people think of her.

   c) her medical bills.

5. Ella thinks visitors will

   a) tell her the truth.

   b) relieve her loneliness.

   c) help her with Henry.

6. Ella imagines death as

   a) a frightening figure.

   b) an old lady.

   c) a friend.

3 *Getting the Joke*

Read each item and decide which answer explains why the audience laughs. Circle your choice. Then, working in groups, compare your answers. If you agree, discuss the reasons for your choices. If you disagree, discuss your opinions and try to come to an agreement. In each case, there is one choice that best explains the joke.

1. "If she says, 'Oh, we're coming into Pepin now, dear,' he'll say, 'What? You didn't wake me up when we went through Fountain City?' "
   Henry cannot function too well in present time, but when it comes to his train route of over sixty years ago, he does not

   a) forget the smallest detail.

   b) fall asleep.

   c) even try to remember.

2. "But, to Ella, Charlotte's faith in doctors is made of the same stuff as Henry's train trip."
   Ella realizes that the cure that Charlotte hopes for and the train trips that Henry takes are both

   a) exciting.

   b) painful.

   c) imaginary.

3. "They are as familiar to Ella, Charlotte's symptoms are, as all the stops of the *Burlington Zephyr*."
   Ella knows the symptoms as well as the train stops because they are

   a) similar to her own.

   b) repeated to her frequently.

   c) the same as Henry's.

4. "You wouldn't have to say an awful lot. And you wouldn't necessarily have to tell the truth either."
   Ella would not require her visitors to tell the truth probably because she

   a) prefers fantasy.

   b) is used to fantasy.

   c) would not listen very carefully.

4 Reviewing Vocabulary

Fill in each blank with one of these words or expressions. Be sure to use the correct form of the italicized words. Compare your answers with those of a classmate.

look like a fool	*have* a fit
specialist	flower bed
worried sick	bad company
skip	out of order
be cooped up	*symptom*

In the spring, Ella Anderson was always glad to get outdoors to begin planting her

_____. She _____ all winter in the house with her
             1   2

husband, Henry. Although he was usually sweet and was not really very _____,
                                                    3

Henry's mind wandered, and Ella was often lonely. During his imaginary train trips, Ella had to go over to

the window and announce each stop, without _____ any of them. If she left any
                                                 4

towns out or got the stops _____, Henry would be upset.
                            5

Ella's daughter, Charlotte, rarely came to visit. She did not think about her parents' health, but she was

_____ about her own _____. As a result, she spent most
               6   7

of her time going to consult _____.
                              8

Ella was so lonely that one day she decided to invite visitors into her home. She put a sign out in her

garden. When Charlotte heard about the sign, she _____ and called her mother
                                      9

right away. Charlotte believed that the sign made her _____, so she forced her
                                      10

mother to take it down.

5 │ *Interpreting the Characters*

Read the following questions and answers. The answers are not mentioned directly in the story, but it is possible to make good guesses based on your knowledge of the story and of American life. Decide whether each answer is *likely* or *unlikely*. Circle your choice. Then, working in small groups, give reasons for your choices and discuss your opinions. There is no one correct answer, but there is more evidence for some choices than for others.

1. Why doesn't Ella call a doctor when Henry's mind goes off on one of his imaginary train trips?

   a) Ella is afraid that a doctor might try to send Henry to a nursing home or hospital, and she would be all alone.   *likely*   *unlikely*

   b) Ella doesn't believe that there is anything a doctor could do to help Henry.   *likely*   *unlikely*

   c) Ella knows that they would be unable to pay for further medical treatment.   *likely*   *unlikely*

2. Why did Charlotte have a fit when Ella put the sign up in her garden?

   a) She was afraid that Ella might be hurt by some unwelcome visitor.   *likely*   *unlikely*

   b) Charlotte would be embarrassed if anyone saw her father during one of his imaginary trips.   *likely*   *unlikely*

   c) She felt guilty that she did not visit her parents more often.   *likely*   *unlikely*

6 | Retelling the Story

Use these phrases to retell the story in your own words. As you speak, try to include as many details as you can. A different student may want to retell each part.

One day in early spring, Ella Anderson was cleaning out her flower bed . . .

This information may help you:

- bad hip
- can't navigate on ice
- cooped up inside since Thanksgiving
- moves slowly around flower beds
- new stand-up technique of gardening
- afraid of not being able to get up
- does not want to ask for help

It's lonely in the house with Henry month after month . . .

- not such bad company
- lies on the couch
- thinks he is on the *Burlington Zephyr* from Chicago to St. Paul
- Ella has to go to a window
- describe the view, name the town
- if she skips a stop, he knows
- if Charlotte were there, an emergency

One day, Ella put a sign out in her flower bed . . .

- "Visitors Welcome"
- Neighbors telephoned Charlotte.
- Charlotte had a fit.
- look like a fool
- Take the sign down.
- worried sick about herself

Ella would like some visitors . . .

- wouldn't have to stay long or say a lot
- would make problems more ordinary
- could imagine death as a friend
- "I'm ready to go."
- friend is Death
- "I think my legs fell asleep."

7 *Telling Your Own Stories*

1 Find out which classmates have had the following experiences. Ask yes/no questions: for example, "Have you known somebody who was able to grow old gracefully, to accept and even enjoy old age?" Try to find one classmate for each statement. When you get a "yes" answer, write that classmate's name in the blank. Do not tell any stories yet. To begin the exercise, stand up and move around the classroom freely.

1. _____ has known somebody who was able to grow old gracefully,
   (name)   to accept and even enjoy old age.

2. _____ has something that he or she likes to do when loneliness
   (name)   makes things seem difficult.

3. _____ knows a hypochondriac, a person who is worried sick
   (name)   about his or her own health.

4. _____ prefers not to go to doctors.
   (name)

2 Look at your list above. If several of you have stories for each experience, one of you should volunteer to be the storyteller. You can tell your stories to the whole class or to small groups. If almost everyone has a story to tell, you might want to work in pairs and exchange stories.

8 Getting into the Language

A Notice the Structure: Modal Perfects

> "Oh yes, it does. It looks like Fountain City. Yes, I **should have recognized** it myself, dear. Beautiful town."

Modal perfects, which are forms of modal auxiliary verbs, are used with past participles to refer to actions in the past. They refer to actions that were possible or advisable but were not accomplished; or they express strong deductions.

***should (not) have* + past participle** Refers to an advisable or obligatory action that was not accomplished.	Ella has given Henry the same train trip many times, so she **should not have forgotten** the stops. (It was not advisable to skip a stop.) She **should have made** herself a list. (It would have been a good idea to write the stops down, but Ella did not do it.)
***could have* + past participle** Refers to a possible action that was not taken.	Instead of working alone, Ella **could have hired** somebody to help her with the gardening. (Hiring somebody was a possibility, but Ella did not do it.)
***could not have* + past participle** Refers to an action that one was unable to take, a physical or logical impossibility.	Henry **could not have helped** Ella with the gardening. (Henry was physically unable to do it.) Henry remembers the year 1917 very clearly. Ella **could not have been** with him then. (This is impossible because she was a young girl and lived in a different area.)

must (not) have + **past participle**
Refers to a strong inference or deduction.

Henry knows the route of the *Burlington Zephyr* very well. When he was younger, Henry **must have taken** that train many times. (It is clear that the memory comes from experience.)

Charlotte is not fully aware of her father's mental condition. Ella **must not have told** her about the train trips. (She does not know, so we deduce that Ella has not informed her.)

B Practice the Structure

1 Charlotte heard about Ella's sign from a neighbor, so she called her mother. Imagine the telephone conversation between Charlotte and Ella. Choose the correct modal perfect and combine it with the past participle of the verb in parentheses to complete each sentence.

CHARLOTTE: Mother, how could you do this to me? You're just trying to embarrass me, to make me look like a fool in front of other people.

ELLA: Well, maybe you're right. Maybe I *shouldn't have put*

                                 1. should not have/must not have (put)

the sign out before talking to you.

CHARLOTTE: Maybe? What do you mean by "maybe"? Of course, you

_____ me. I come to see you as often as
    2. should have/must have (consult)

I can. You easily _____ yesterday and
                       3. could have/must have (call)

asked me to visit you.

ELLA: Yes, dear. I suppose we _____ all this
                        4. could have/must have (avoid)

fuss with a simple phone call.

CHARLOTTE: Now go out and take that sign down. Please take it down, Mother. Things like this have happened before. You just weren't thinking. When the neighbors saw that sign, they

_____ that I never visit you at all.
    5. should have/must have (think)

ELLA: All right, dear. I guess I will. It will take me a little while, though, because my hip has been very stiff lately.

2 Use your own ideas and information from the story to answer each question. Write complete sentences with the expressions in parentheses.

1. When Charlotte had a fit, her mother took the sign down. What else could Ella have done? (could have)

_____

2. Charlotte could not have allowed Ella to keep her sign up. Why not? (could not have)

_____

3. Ella did not have any tulips in her flower bed this year. Did she plant any? (must not have)

_____

4. After a day of gardening, Ella had a sharp pain in her arm. What must have happened while she was working? (must have)

_____

5. Ella embarrassed Charlotte with her sign. What does Charlotte think about Ella's behavior now? (should have)

_____

9 *Extending the Story in Writing*

A *Writing Down a Story*

Write down a story from Exercise 7, either one you heard or your own. If you choose another student's story, show your work to the storyteller when you finish. Ask the storyteller to comment on your version. Then revise the story, making any necessary changes and corrections.

B *Keeping a Journal*

Have you ever kept a journal of your thoughts and feelings? This highly personal kind of writing takes many forms, although most journal keepers share a preference for the first person and make a habit of writing at regular intervals.

Joan Didion, a writer from California, explains how she uses her journal:

So the point of my keeping a notebook has never been, nor is it now, to have an accurate factual record of what I have been doing or thinking . . . .

How it felt to me: that is getting closer to the truth about a notebook.

I imagine in other words, that the notebook is about other people. But of course it is not. . . .

Remember what it was to be me: that is always the point.

Model

Ella Anderson thinks of her journal as a silent friend. Every evening, after Henry goes to sleep, she sits at the kitchen table with a tablet of lined paper and writes down the things she cannot say out loud. This is one of her recent journal entries:

> Sunday, May 4th
>
> Tonight I'm really exhausted after a rough "trip" with Henry. Sometimes he can be hard on me. "What? Did you skip Fountain City? Why didn't you wake me up?" But how can I complain? His mind is floating free; he cannot know what tricks it is playing on him.
>
> I've been thinking about my garden. I should have ordered the seeds earlier, but I was too worried about Henry. Anyway, a beautiful flower bed will raise my spirits, especially after being cooped up indoors all winter. Tomorrow I must get down to the Feed 'n' Seed to buy a trowel and some garden gloves. Do I dare call Charlotte to take me? Can I bear to hear her list of symptoms again?
>
> Monday, May 5th
>
> It was a painful day. We made an early run to Chicago, no skipped stops. Henry must have felt happy that I got him to Chicago on time, but by noon I felt I would lose my mind if I couldn't talk to somebody. I could have just called Charlotte, but I made the bold decision to put up a sign in the garden inviting people in....

Assignment

1. Complete Ella Anderson's journal entry for May 5th. Then write one for the following day. Try to imagine, as Joan Didion says, "how it felt to be Ella." Use the structures and vocabulary from the unit.

2. Begin keeping a journal of your own. Sit down to write at the same time and in the same place each day. If you would like somebody else to read it, exchange journals with a classmate. Then, if you wish, hand it in to your teacher.

UNIT 11
Uncle Ed, the Norwegian Bachelor Farmer

1 | *Judging from Experience*

Read the question. Discuss the answers with your classmates.

Look at the drawing. Who might this old man be, and why is the family coming out to greet him?

Part One

A *Vocabulary*

Read the sentences and find the word or expression in the box that means the same as the italicized words. Then compare your answers with those of a classmate. If you disagree, consult another classmate, a dictionary or your teacher.

1. _____ Many different *firms* can have their offices in one building.

2. _____ A simple *operation* can be done in the doctor's office.

3. _____ People who live in the countryside wonder how others *put up with* the noise and dirt of the city.

4. _____ The sink was so full that some water *splashed* onto the floor.

5. _____ *Wintergreen* is an old-fashioned type of men's cologne.

6. _____ For special celebrations, people often go out for *a night on the town*.

7. _____ Children may feel *ashamed* when they are corrected by their parents in public.

8. _____ Although it is a very old verb form, *ain't* is not considered correct standard English.

9. _____ Sometimes it is necessary to give the *maitre d'* a tip to get a good table at a restaurant.

10. _____ Sometimes it is better not to interfere in other people's problems. After all, *that's their business*.

a) tolerate, stand

b) businesses

c) fell in drops

d) fresh-smelling, mint-like oil

e) an evening of dining or entertainment at restaurants or clubs

f) cutting of the body to remove a diseased part

g) host who greets diners at a restaurant

h) what they are doing is private

i) embarrassed

j) am not, is not, are not, has not, have not

B Getting the Gist of the Story 🔲

This is a story about Tina Tollefson and her Uncle Ed, an old farmer who came to Minnesota from Norway when he was young. He has never married, so he lives alone on his farm outside of Lake Wobegon.

Listen to Part One of the story. Read the question and write your answer. Then compare your answer with those of a classmate.

1. Why did Uncle Ed have to come down to the city?

_____ _____

_____

2. Why did Tina decide to take Uncle Ed out for a night on the town?

_____

_____

C Listening for Detail 🔲

Listen again to Part One. Circle the letter of the answer that best completes each sentence. Then compare your answers with those of a classmate. Listen again if you disagree with each other.

1. Tina Tollefson is married to a

   a) lawyer.

   b) psychologist.

   c) schoolteacher.

2. Tina and her husband live

   a) with her mother.

   b) alone.

   c) with their youngest child.

3. Tina's mother drove Uncle Ed down to the city

   a) on Monday.

   b) on Friday.

   c) two weeks ago.

4. Uncle Ed's way of farming is

   a) unhealthy.

   b) neat.

   c) old-fashioned.

5. Uncle Ed takes a bath _____ other people do.

   a) less often than

   b) more often than

   c) as often as

6. Uncle Ed had _____ come to the city before.

   a) frequently

   b) never

   c) rarely

7. Tina and her husband took Uncle Ed for a
_____ around the lakes in their
neighborhood.

a) walk

b) run

c) drive

8. The shoes Uncle Ed wore to the restaurant
were

a) inappropriate.

b) fancy.

c) new.

Part One

$\boxed{D}$ Vocabulary

1 Read the sentences and find the word or expression in the box that means the
same as the italicized words. Then compare your answers with those of a
classmate. If you disagree, consult another classmate, a dictionary or your teacher.

1. _____ An actor's voice must *carry* very well so that he or she can be heard
throughout the theater.

2. _____ The child *snuck* a cookie while the mother was not watching.

3. _____ At a *salad bar,* customers can make exactly the kind of salad that they
want.

4. _____ Cold *macaroni salad* is a common summertime food.

5. _____ With so many hungry people in the world, it is *a shame* that
restaurants throw out so much food.

6. _____ At a summer picnic, each person might eat more than one *ear* of corn.

7. _____ Horses like to eat *hay.*

8. _____ In the spring, farmers go out in the fields and *cultivate.*

9. _____ For soldiers at war, the battlefield is a *hellhole.*

a) terrible place
b) prepare the soil for growing
c) secretly took
d) travel
e) cut, dried grass
f) an unfortunate thing
g) a table full of the ingredients for making a salad
h) a salad made with a type of small noodle
i) the part of the corn plant that contains the pieces we eat

2 Circle the letter of the expression that is closest in meaning to the italicized word or phrase. Then compare your answers with those of a classmate.

1. Because many old people become *hard of hearing,* it can be frustrating to have a conversation with them.

   a) quiet   **b)** deaf   **c)** difficult

2. Breakfast at an inexpensive restaurant should not be more than a few *bucks.*

   a) dollars   **b)** cents   **c)** eggs

3. The soup was too strong, so the cook *watered it down.*

   a) boiled it   **b)** threw it away   **c)** added water to it

4. When a baby sees its mother, it usually *grins.*

   a) cries   **b)** smiles   **c)** eats

5. Some people like to sit in a café and *carry on* a conversation for hours.

   a) have   **b)** listen to   **c)** remember

6. At a big dinner with many courses, the guests can *keep on* eating for hours.

   a) try   **b)** think about   **c)** continue

7. When you order a new kind of food at a restaurant, *there's no telling* whether you will like it or not.

   a) it is impossible to know   **b)** no one says   **c)** you should not guess

8. After a big meal, sometimes it feels good to leave the table and *take a nap.*

   a) use a napkin   **b)** take a shower   **c)** sleep for a little while

$\boxed{E}$ *Predicting and Listening* 🔲

1 Working in small groups. discuss the question. Predict what might happen next in the story. Write down at least two possible answers.

What will happen with Uncle Ed, Tina, her husband, and their son at the restaurant?

a. _____

_____

b. _____

_____

c. _____

_____

2 Keeping your same groups, listen to the end of the story. Discuss how your predictions were different from the ending you heard.

F Listening for Detail

Listen again to Part Two. Circle the letter of the answer that best completes each sentence. Then compare your answers with those of a classmate. Listen again if you disagree with each other.

1. The maitre d' at the restaurant gave Tina and her family a table

   a) in the kitchen.

   b) in the corner.

   c) near the window.

2. The kitchen workers at the restaurant could _____ Uncle Ed.

   a) hear

   b) see

   c) talk to

3. When Uncle Ed got his drink, he _____ the ice cubes.

   a) chewed

   b) took out

   c) played with

4. Tina's husband was _____ by Uncle Ed's behavior.

   a) amused

   b) confused

   c) embarrassed

5. Tina's son was _____ by his father's behavior.

   a) embarrassed

   b) confused

   c) amused

6. When other people in the restaurant looked at Uncle Ed, Tina

   a) did nothing.

   b) stared back.

   c) got up.

7. Uncle Ed _____ macaroni salad.

   a) did not eat any

   b) ate a little bit of

   c) ate a lot of

8. Uncle Ed _____ his broiled fish.

   a) complained about

   b) enjoyed

   c) returned

9. Tina talked to Uncle Ed about

   a) their family history.

   b) the meal.

   c) his operation.

10. The doctors said that in six months or a year, Uncle Ed

    a) should come back to the hospital.

    b) might die.

    c) should go home.

11. Uncle Ed's horses, Queenie and Gus, understand

    a) only French.

    b) only English.

    c) only Norwegian.

12. Uncle Ed told his horses that some of the people in the city were

    a) friendly.

    b) happy.

    c) not bad.

3 Getting the Joke

Read each item and decide which answer explains why the audience laughs. Circle your choice. Then, working in groups, compare your answers. If you agree, discuss the reasons for your choices. If you disagree, discuss your opinions and try to come to an agreement. In each case, there is one choice that best explains the joke.

1. "Tina Tollefson came down here and went to college, married a boy who sat next to her in psychology class, to whom she always gave the answers. She gave him enough good ones so that he got into law school."
   This comment implies that Tina

   a) knew her husband better than he knew her.

   b) should have become a psychologist.

   c) was more intelligent than her husband.

2. "Uncle Ed is one of what we call Norwegian bachelor farmers . . . Lives by himself. Keeps his place fairly neat, according to his own standards."
   An old farmer who lives alone probably thinks that neatness is

   a) very important.

   b) not so important.

   c) a private matter.

3. "He was kind of curious about people running around the lakes. 'What were they doing?' She said, 'They're doing that for exercise, Uncle Ed.' He said, 'That's kind of dumb, ain't it? Why don't they get work? Why don't they get jobs?' "
   In Uncle Ed's opinion, any worthwhile job

   a) requires physical exercise.

   b) is more important than exercise.

   c) is easy to find.

4. "Tina's husband was looking off at the ceiling, he was looking off at the walls, as if he didn't know these people, they'd just come in, they'd been seated at his table, he was not with them. This was not happening. The boy sat there grinning. He'd never seen his dad so embarrassed. He wanted to see more of it."
   The boy's dad is usually

   a) shy.

   b) comfortable.

   c) observant.

5. "When Uncle Ed said, 'They sure give you small plates, don't they?' she said, 'Yes, they do!' "

   Tina _____ that the plates were so small.

   a) had always thought but had never said

   b) had never thought about the fact

   c) did not really agree

4 Reviewing Vocabulary

Fill in each blank with one of these words or expressions. Be sure to use the correct form of the italicized words. Compare your answers with those of a classmate.

put up with	shame	there *be* no telling
that's *one's* business	grin	take a nap
carry on	ashamed	*keep* on
a night on the town	*be* hard of hearing	

Uncle Ed is one of those old men whom the people in Lake Wobegon call a Norwegian bachelor farmer. He recently had to come down to a Minneapolis hospital for an operation. Tina Tollefson received a call from her mother, who asked her if she could _____ (1) Uncle Ed for a few days before the operation. She agreed, and because it was his first trip to the city, Tina decided to take him out to a restaurant downtown for _____ (2). Tina's husband was _____ (3) to be seen with this old man who had uncombed hair and spoke in a loud voice because he _____ (4). At the restaurant, the other diners _____ (5) staring at Tina and her family, but she refused to let it bother her. She thought, "Well, if they don't like it, _____ (6)!" While she _____ (7) a conversation with Uncle Ed, her husband was becoming more and more embarrassed. This delighted their son, and made him _____ (8) while he watched his dad. Uncle Ed complained about his dinner, saying that it was a _____ (9) to put a sauce on a piece of fish.

Uncle Ed had his operation, and after seeing the doctors, he was sent home to Lake Wobegon. The doctors told Tina that _____ (10) how long Uncle Ed might live, perhaps six months or a year.

When Uncle Ed got home, he was glad to see his horses, Queenie and Gus. After feeding them some oats, corn and hay, he told them that he was going to _____ (11). He also said that although he hated the city, some of the people there were not bad.

5 | *Interpreting the Characters*

Read the following questions and answers. The answers are not mentioned directly in the story, but it is possible to make good guesses based on your knowledge of the story and of American life. Decide whether each answer is *likely* or *unlikely*. Circle your choice. Then, working in small groups, give reasons for your choices and discuss your opinions. There is no one correct answer, but there is more evidence for some choices than for others.

1. Why did Tina's husband suggest that Uncle Ed would not enjoy going out for a night on the town?

    a) He thought that Uncle Ed was too sick to go out.   *likely*   *unlikely*

    b) He thought that Uncle Ed would embarrass the   *likely*   *unlikely*
    family.

    c) He did not want to spend a lot of money on an old   *likely*   *unlikely*
    farmer who would not appreciate it.

2. Why did Tina keep on talking while her Uncle Ed continued complaining about the meal?

    a) She hoped people would stop staring at Ed if they   *likely*   *unlikely*
    thought he was having a conversation with her.

    b) She agreed with all of Uncle Ed's criticisms.   *likely*   *unlikely*

    c) She wanted to show Uncle Ed that she loved him.   *likely*   *unlikely*

6 | Retelling the Story

Use these phrases to retell the story in your own words. As you speak, try to include as many details as you can. A different student may want to retell each part.

This information may help you:

Tina Tollefson moved down to the city from Lake Wobegon twenty-some years ago . . .

- went to college
- the boy next to her in psychology class
- law school
- nice house
- one child left

Her mother wrote to her . . .

- Uncle Ed
- operation
- put up with him
- Norwegian bachelor farmer
- Queenie and Gus
- fairly neat
- takes a bath

Tina decided to take Uncle Ed out . . .

- a night on the town
- ashamed
- running around the lakes
- get jobs
- maitre d' at the restaurant
- well-dressed family
- work boots, hair not combed
- hard of hearing
- voice carries
- ice cubes
- Tina's husband
- son grinning
- snuck a stare
- salad bar
- broiled fish
- kept on talking

Uncle Ed came out of the hospital on Friday . . .

- six months or a year
- there's no telling
- horses waiting for him
- speak Norwegian
- hellhole
- take a nap
- cultivate

7 Telling Your Own Stories

1 Find out which classmates have had the following experiences. Ask yes/no questions: for example, "Do you often go out for a night on the town?" Try to find one classmate for each statement. When you get a "yes" answer, write that classmate's name in the blank. Do not tell any stories yet. To begin the exercise, stand up and move around the classroom freely.

1. _____ often goes out for a night on the town.
    (name)

2. _____ has felt embarrassed by the behavior of a relative.
    (name)

3. _____ has helped someone who was going to die soon.
    (name)

4. _____ has done some sort of hard physical work.
    (name)

2 Look at your list above. If several of you have stories for each experience, one of you should volunteer to be the storyteller. You can tell your stories to the whole class or to small groups. If almost everyone has a story to tell, you might want to work in pairs and exchange stories.

8 Getting into the Language

A Notice the Structures: the Past Perfect versus the Simple Past

> "The boy **sat** there grinning. He **had** never **seen** his dad so embarrassed."

As you learned in Unit 6, the past perfect tense is used to refer to an action that came before another action or event in the past. Look at the example above. At the restaurant, the boy enjoyed his father's embarrassment. He sat there and grinned. Notice that the simple past tense is used here. His father had been embarrassed before, but never so much as at that dinner. The past perfect is used to refer to the boy's experience with his father before that evening.

B Practice the Structure

Fill in the blanks in the following passage with either a simple past tense form or with a past perfect tense form of the verb in parentheses.

When Tina, her husband and son _____ with Uncle Ed to their favorite
                                        (1. go)

restaurant downtown, the maitre d' _____ them a table in the corner behind a palm
                                            (2. give)

tree. In the past, they always _____ a nice big table by the window. When they
                                        (3. have)

_____ Uncle Ed out, they _____ embarrassed when other
        (4. take)   (5. feel)

people _____ at them. However, on earlier occasions, they always
            (6. stare)

_____ pleased to see other people at the restaurant. Tina's husband
        (7. be)

_____ embarrassed, but Tina did not mind talking with Uncle Ed. As a matter of
        (8. be)

fact, until Uncle Ed _____ something about the salad plates, Tina never
                                (9. say)

_____ anything about how small they were.
        (10. say)

9 Extending the Story in Writing

A Writing Down a Story

Write down a story from Exercise 7, either one you heard or your own. If you
choose another student's story, show your work to the storyteller when you finish.
Ask the storyteller to comment on your version. Then revise the story, making
any necessary changes and corrections.

B Writing a Conversation

Model

A few days after Uncle Ed had his operation and was brought home again, Tina
called her mother and told her all about her visit with Uncle Ed. Here is the
beginning of their conversation. Notice that Tina and her mother use both the
simple past tense and the past perfect tense.

MOTHER: Hello?

TINA: Hi, Mom. It's Tina.

MOTHER: Yes, how are you, dear?

TINA: Oh, fine. I was wondering about Uncle Ed. You know, before he
          stayed with us that weekend, I had never understood him very
          well. He's a very interesting man, isn't he? How's he feeling?

MOTHER: Well, honey, I had planned to call you the other day, but it got
          very late. So I'm glad you called . . .

Assignment

Write the rest of the conversation between Tina and her mother. Using what you know about the characters of Uncle Ed and Tina, imagine what her mother might be like and what she would say. Be sure to include the following information. Use these phrases in sentences that also contain verbs in the past perfect tense. You may also want to use reported speech (see Exercises 9 in Unit 5).

- before Uncle Ed went to the doctor last month . . .
- before we came down to the city last week . . .
- before we went to the restaurant downtown . . .
- before Uncle Ed went into the hospital for his operation . . .
- before we left Uncle Ed back at the farm again . . .

UNIT 12

Mr. Turnblad Makes His Dream Come True

1 Judging from Experience

Read the questions. Discuss the answers with your classmates.

1. Look at the top drawing. What do you imagine the people with gunny sacks are thinking about as they gather the farmer's potatoes?
2. What do you think the farmer is daydreaming about as he rides across his potato field?
3. Look at the bottom drawing. What do you think is happening in the barn?

2 Listening

Part One

A Vocabulary

1 Read the sentences and find the word or expression in the box that means the same as the italicized words. Then compare your answers with those of a classmate. If you disagree, consult another classmate, a dictionary or your teacher.

1. _____ If a traveler wants to sail across the ocean in an elegant style, he or she might go on *an ocean-going yacht*.

2. _____ Some people who read travel books *think of themselves as* explorers even though they rarely take any trips.

3. _____ *Evidently* a good travel story can be almost as exciting as an actual trip.

4. _____ In adventure books, such as those by Richard Haliburton or Richard Henry Dana, the sea captain often finds himself *at the helm in heavy swells*.

5. _____ If you imagine yourself sailing on the ocean, you can almost feel the cool *spray* from the waves.

6. _____ Cedar and oak *lumber* was used to make beautiful old sailing ships.

7. _____ When a boat is being built, the first part to be completed is the *hull*.

8. _____ After the boat's hull is built, the *deck* is added on top.

9. _____ The mother rocked her newborn baby in the *crook* of her arm.

a) consider themselves

b) bend

c) main body of a boat

d) drops of water carried in the wind

e) it seems that

f) a large boat strong enough to sail on the ocean

g) platform extending from one side of a boat to another

h) wood cut into boards

i) steering a boat in large open-ocean waves

2 Circle the letter of the expression that is closest in meaning to the italicized word or phrase. Then compare your answers with those of a classmate.

1. Teenagers are often hired to help gather the potato crop. The problem for the farmer is that they cannot *keep up with* the experienced workers.

   a) work as many months as   **b)** move as quickly as

   c) make as much money as

2. People *assume* that younger workers will be faster than older ones, but this is not always true.

   a) suppose   **b)** know   **c)** read

3. If a barn is too old, the farmer might *tear it down* and build a new one, rather than repair it.

   a) burn it down   **b)** move it away   **c)** destroy it completely

4. I am very excited. To complete my degree in English literature, I lack *but* two courses.

   a) only   **b)** less than   **c)** more than

5. Some of us felt sick as the high waves made the boat *pitch*.

   a) sink   **b)** roll   **c)** stop

6. Most farmers hope that, after they retire, their children will *take over* and run the farm.

   a) rebuild   **b)** buy   **c)** start to manage

B | Getting the Gist of the Story 🔊

This is a story about Mr. Turnblad, a Minnesota potato farmer in his late sixties, who was a dreamer.

Listen to Part One of the story. After you listen, write your answers to the questions.

1. What was Mr. Turnblad's dream?

_____

2. What did he do about it?

_____

Listen again to Part One. Circle the letter of the answer that best completes the sentence. Then compare your answers with those of a classmate. Listen again if you disagree with each other.

1. Mr. Turnblad dreamed of constructing

   a) another potato barn.

   b) a large boat.

   c) his own potato digger.

2. The storyteller, Garrison Keillor, thought of Mr. Turnblad as a

   a) man of the sea.

   b) guy who rode up and down on a tractor and yelled at the workers

   c) kid who dragged a gunny sack and picked potatoes.

3. Mr. Turnblad didn't think of himself as a

   a) farmer in overalls.

   b) secret reader of adventure books.

   c) sea captain.

4. The ocean spray that Mr. Turnblad imagined was actually

   a) flying insects.

   b) light rain.

   c) dust from the field.

5. The farm workers filled the frame in Mr. Turnblad's barn with

   a) lumber.

   b) water.

   c) potatoes.

6. When the hull cracked, Mr. Turnblad

   a) cried.

   b) yelled.

   c) left.

7. When they tore down the potato barn,

   a) Mr. Turnblad was bothered.

   b) Mr. Turnblad's son Wilmer was upset.

   c) the children were happy.

8. Mr. Turnblad intended to be away from home

   a) for a morning.

   b) for the whole summer.

   c) forever.

Part Two

D Vocabulary

Circle the letter of the expression that is closest in meaning to the italicized word or phrase. Then compare your answers with those of a classmate.

1. In order to sail a boat, you must learn how to operate all of the *rigging*.

   a) ropes and sails   **b)** plumbing   **c)** lights

2. All of your questions about the parts and operation of a sailboat can be answered quickly and clearly by a good *manual*.

   a) handbook   **b)** lecture   **c)** magazine

3. Because of the warm climate, many retired people go to Florida to *settle*.

   a) visit   **b)** live   **c)** swim

4. It is so sunny at the beach that you have to buy a pair of dark *shades*.

   a) pants   **b)** sunglasses   **c)** shoes

5. A few weeks in the sun and ocean air can make a person look and feel *awfully* healthy.

   a) somewhat   **b)** unexpectedly   **c)** very

6. People who do difficult physical work often become *lean and muscular*.

   a) sick and tired   **b)** tall and tan   **c)** thin and strong-looking

7. Many people in the Florida Keys are in the business of *chartering* boats to tourists for short fishing trips.

   a) selling   **b)** renting   **c)** recommending

E Predicting and Listening

1 Working in small groups, discuss the question. Predict what might happen next in the story. Write down at least two possible answers.

How will Mr. Turnblad be able to fulfill his dream of becoming a man of the sea?

a. _____

b. _____

c. _____

2 Keeping your same groups, listen to the end of the story. Discuss how your predictions were different from the ending you heard.

F Listening for Detail

Listen again to Part Two. Circle the letter of the answer that best completes the sentence. Then compare your answers with those of a classmate. Listen again if you disagree with each other.

1. Mr. Turnblad learned how to sail

   a) on Lake Wobegon.

   b) from his son Wilmer.

   c) as he headed out into the Gulf of Mexico.

2. In the photo that Mr. Turnblad sent, the family could not see his

   a) chest.

   b) eyes.

   c) face.

3. In the photo, Mr. Turnblad was not wearing

   a) glasses.

   b) a smile.

   c) a shirt.

4. Wilmer died of a heart attack while he was

   a) fishing.

   b) farming.

   c) heading down to Florida.

5. To earn money in Marathon, Mr. Turnblad started to

   a) fish.

   b) rent his boat.

   c) farm.

6. Mr. Turnblad's curiosity about the sea was satisfied after he

   a) sailed to the Bahamas.

   b) crossed the Atlantic Ocean.

   c) made it to the Florida Keys.

3 | *Getting the Joke*

Read each item and decide which answer explains why the audience laughs. Circle your choice. Then, working in groups, compare your answers. If you agree, discuss the reasons for your choices. If you disagree, discuss your opinions and try to come to an agreement. In each case, there is one choice that best explains the joke.

1. "Mr. Turnblad thought of himself as a captain who lacked but two things: just a boat and an ocean."
   People in town probably did not think of him this way. They probably thought of him as a potato farmer because he

   a) rarely talked about the ocean.

   b) looked and acted like a potato farmer.

   c) seemed to really enjoy potato farming.

2. "They had to tear down the potato barn to get the boat out, but that didn't bother Mr. Turnblad. . . It kind of bothered his son Wilmer, who was taking over the farm."
   Wilmer was bothered by the fact that his father was leaving. But, since he was taking over the farm, Wilmer was probably much more upset that his father was

   a) becoming a sailor

   b) behaving angrily toward him.

   c) destroying something Wilmer needed.

3. "Those dark glasses seemed to say: 'You don't really know me at all.' And that smile on his face said: 'Don't expect me back anytime soon.' "
   Mr. Turnblad probably sent this photograph back home to his family to show them that he

   a) had arrived safely in Florida.

   b) was thinking of them.

   c) had completely changed.

4 Reviewing Vocabulary

Fill in each blank with one of these words or expressions. Be sure to use the correct form of the italicized words. Compare your answers with those of a classmate.

ocean-going yacht	*assume*
tear down	lean and muscular
manual	*think* of *oneself* as
charter	*take* over
settle	evidently

Mr. Turnblad was a potato farmer in Lake Wobegon who _____ a man of the

1

sea. Working for several years, he built an _____ in his potato barn. Because it

2

was too big to fit through the barn door, he _____ the barn to get it out. Since

3

Wilmer _____ the farm, he was upset by this. _____ Mr.

4   5

Turnblad did not care anymore because he intended to sail down the Mississippi River, and then head out

into the Gulf of Mexico. He did not ever plan to go back to farming.

One day in May, Mr. Turnblad put his boat in the river. Although he had never sailed before, he

_____ he could learn how from a _____ on the subject.

6   7

He must have taught himself fairly well, as he made it to the Florida Keys, and eventually

_____ in Marathon. Not long after, he sent a photograph of himself, looking

8

_____, back home to his family in Lake Wobegon. He told them that he had gone

9

into the business of _____ his fishing boat, and that he did not expect them to

10

understand his new life.

5 | *Interpreting the Characters*

Read the following questions and answers. The answers are not mentioned directly in the story, but it is possible to make good guesses based on your knowledge of the story and of American life. Decide whether each answer is *likely* or *unlikely*. Circle your choice. Then, working in groups, give reasons for your choices and discuss your opinions. There is no one correct answer, but there is more evidence for some choices than for others.

1. Wilmer, who was taking over the farm, was upset when his father tore down the potato barn to get his boat out. Why do you think that Mr. Turnblad was not particularly upset?

a) He figured that the farm belonged to Wilmer and that it had become his problem now.   *likely*   *unlikely*

b) He had become a sea captain, and he actually enjoyed seeing the barn come down.   *likely*   *unlikely*

c) After all of his hard work building the boat, he knew that rebuilding the barn would be easy.   *likely*   *unlikely*

2. Mr. Turnblad went back to Minnesota for his son's funeral in the summer, but he didn't stay long. Why do you think that he went right back to Florida?

a) He wanted to leave Minnesota before the cold weather returned.   *likely*   *unlikely*

b) His new life in Florida was simply more important to him. He had completely changed his life.   *likely*   *unlikely*

c) It scared him to think that if he had continued farming, he might have died early, too.   *likely*   *unlikely*

6 | Retelling the Story

Use these phrases to retell the story in your own words. As you speak, try to include as many details as you can. A different student may want to retell each part.

This information may help you:

Mr. Turnblad, a Minnesota potato farmer, thought of himself as . . .

- little guy in overalls
- man of the sea
- captain without a boat or an ocean
- secret reader
- tractor like a boat
- dust like ocean spray

One year, Mr. Turnblad began to build an ocean-going yacht in his potato barn . . .

- hull filled with potatoes
- Mr. Turnblad cried
- rebuilt the boat
- tore down the barn
- Wilmer upset
- to New Orleans and out into the Gulf of Mexico
- a manual on sailing

When Mr. Turnblad got to the Florida Keys, he decided to settle in Marathon . . .

- photo
- captain's hat and shades
- lean and muscular
- "don't expect me back anytime soon"
- charter boat business
- Wilmer's funeral
- went right back to Florida
- thought about the Bahamas or England
- curiosity was satisfied

7 | Telling Your Own Stories

1 Find out which classmates have had the following experiences. Ask yes/no questions: for example, "Were you influenced by a book that you read as a child?" Try to find one classmate for each statement. When you get a "yes" answer, write that classmate's name in the blank. Do not tell any stories yet. To begin the exercise, stand up and move around the classroom freely.

1. _____ was influenced by a book that he or she read as a child.
      (name)

2. _____ has realized, or fulfilled, a dream or an ambition.
      (name)

3. _____ went on a journey that changed his or her outlook on life.
      (name)

4. _____ dreams about having a new life in a new place.
      (name)

2 Look at your list above. If several of you have stories for each experience, one of you should volunteer to be the storyteller. You can tell your stories to the whole class or to small groups. If almost everyone has a story to tell, you might want to work in pairs and exchange stories.

8 | Getting into the Language

A | Notice the Structure: Adjective Clauses

> Mr. Turnblad, **whom I knew as a boy,** built an ocean-going yacht in his potato barn. I always thought of him as the little guy in overalls **who rode on the Farm-All.**

Adjective clauses are used to identify, describe or provide more information about the nouns that they modify. They are often introduced by a relative pronoun: *who, whom, which, that, whose.* If the adjective clause identifies the noun and is essential to the meaning of the sentence, it is called a restrictive clause. However, if it adds information that is simply descriptive, it is called a nonrestrictive clause and is enclosed in commas.

Restrictive Adjective Clauses

If the relative pronoun is the subject of the adjective clause:

- use *who* or *that* to refer to people.

  Wilmer was the son **who** was going to take over the farm. (Wilmer was the son. Wilmer was going to take over the farm.)

- use *which* or *that* to refer to things.

  The barn **which** was torn down belonged to Wilmer. (The barn was torn down. The barn belonged to Wilmer.)

If the relative pronoun is the object of the adjective clause:

- use *whom* or *that* to refer to people; or omit the relative pronoun.

  The Mr. Turnblad [that] we knew never would have taken his shirt off. (We knew Mr. Turnblad. He never would have taken his shirt off.)

- use *which* or *that* to refer to things; or omit the relative pronoun.

  The problem [that] Wilmer had was a lack of storage space for potatoes. (Wilmer had a problem. The problem was a lack of storage space for potatoes.)

If the relative pronoun indicates possession:

- use *whose* for a person or thing.

  The person **whose** barn was destroyed was upset. (The person was upset. The person's barn was destroyed.)

  This was a boat **whose** rigging was somewhat unusual. (This was a boat with rigging. The boat's rigging was somewhat unusual.)

Nonrestrictive Adjective Clauses (These are enclosed in commas. In these clauses, *that* cannot be used as a relative pronoun, and relative pronouns cannot be omitted.)

If the relative pronoun is the subject of the clause:

- use *who* to refer to people.

Wilmer, **who** was 35 years old, had not expected his father to leave. (Wilmer was 35 years old. Wilmer had not expected his father to leave.)

- use *which* to refer to things.

Mr. Turnblad's departure, **which** shocked everybody, was the first step in the fulfillment of his dream. (Mr. Turnblad's departure shocked everybody. Mr. Turnblad's departure was the first step in the fulfillment of his dream.)

If the relative pronoun is the object of the clause:

- use *whom* to refer to people

Wilmer, **whom** we had known for years, was a quiet, hardworking man. (We had known Wilmer for years. Wilmer was a quiet, hardworking man.)

- use *which* to refer to things

Mr. Turnblad's photo, **which** surprised us, was taken by one of his new friends. (We were surprised by the photo. Mr. Turnblad's photo was taken by one of his new friends.)

If the relative pronoun indicates possession:

- use *whose* for a person or thing.

Richard Haliburton, **whose** books were an inspiration for Mr. Turnblad, is well known for his adventure writing. (Richard Haliburton is well known for his adventure writing. His books were an inspiration to Mr. Turnblad.)

The sailing manual, **whose** every page Mr. Turnblad learned by heart, remained nailed to the helm throughout the voyage. (The sailing manual remained nailed to the helm. Mr. Turnblad learned every page of the manual by heart.)

B Practice the Structure

1 Write sentences with restrictive adjective clauses. Use the information in parentheses with a relative pronoun: *who, which, that, whom, whose.*

a. Lake Wobegon is a town (Lake Wobegon has produced a lot of dreamers).

Lake Wobegon is a town that has produced a lot of dreamers.

b. Mr. Turnblad was a potato farmer (Mr. Turnblad built an ocean-going yacht in his barn).

_____

c. He thought of himself as a captain (he lacked a boat and an ocean).

_____

d. Mr. Turnblad was a great reader (his favorite books were adventure stories).

_____

e. The people (Mr. Turnblad had hired these people) to pick potatoes could not distinguish between a hull of a boat and a storage bin for potatoes.

_____

f. The boat (Mr. Turnblad built this boat) was almost as large as the potato barn.

_____

2 Write sentences with nonrestrictive adjective clauses. Introduce the clause with one of these relative pronouns: *who, which, whom, whose.* Be sure to enclose the clause in commas.

a. Mr. Turnblad's boat (it had to be hauled to the Mississippi River by a flatbed truck) was launched in May.

Mr. Turnblad's boat, which had to be hauled to the Mississippi River by a flatbed truck, was launched in May.

b. By September, Mr. Turnblad had made it to New Orleans (it is a port on the Gulf of Mexico).

_____

c. The boat (the boat's every feature was known to Mr. Turnblad) must have been seaworthy, since he continued sailing it to the Florida Keys.

_____

d. Mr. Turnblad (he usually avoided having his photograph taken) sent his family a snapshot of himself from Florida.

_____

e. The photograph (it was taken by a friend) showed Mr. Turnblad in a white captain's hat, shades and no shirt.

_____

_____

f. Wilmer (everybody loved him) died of a heart attack.

_____

_____

g. Mr. Turnblad (Mr. Turnblad's original dream had been to cross the Atlantic) later decided not to sail beyond the Florida Keys.

_____

_____

9 Extending the Story in Writing

A Writing Down a Story

Write down a story from Exercise 7, either one you heard or your own. If you choose another student's story, show your work to the storyteller when you finish. Ask the storyteller to comment on your version. Then revise the story, making any necessary changes and corrections.

B Writing a Personal Essay

In personal essays, writers use their own experiences to illustrate a point that others may be able to identify with. Because of the personal nature of the subject, the first person is commonly used. Other than these differences, the structure is the same as that of any essay. There is an introduction containing a thesis statement, several paragraphs of supporting material and a brief conclusion.

Model

Read the first two paragraphs of a personal essay by Gilbert E. Kaplan, a businessman who had an unusual ambition. This essay appeared on the Op-Ed page of the _New York Times,_ a page of opinion pieces, on June 1, 1983.

> Have you ever thought about living out your dream? I have—and some months ago I actually lived one out, a dream that had haunted me for almost two decades. My dream had to do with music, specifically, the "Resurrection Symphony" by Gustav Mahler.

From the first time I heard this symphony, it has had an emotional claim on me, difficult to describe. After years of studying the work, attending every performance I could, listening to every record available, I decided that the only way I could fully experience it was actually to conduct the work. So, I engaged an orchestra and booked Avery Fisher Hall.*

Assignment

Ask yourself Kaplan's question: "Have you ever thought about living our your dream?" Whether you, like Mr. Turnblad and Mr. Kaplan, have already realized your ambition, or whether you are just now planning how to do it, write a personal essay in which you state one of your goals. Then, describe the steps you plan to take, or those you have already taken, in order to fulfill your dream. Use adjective clauses to describe your goal ("a dream that had haunted me for almost two decades") and to characterize yourself (Like Mr. Turnblad, I am the kind of person who . . .).

*The concert hall at Lincoln Center for the Performing Arts in New York City.

Tapescript

UNIT 1   The Living Flag

Part One

Tomorrow is Flag Day in Lake Wobegon. I don't know if it's observed here in the Cities, but it is in Lake Wobegon. The Chamber of Commerce still has some flags on the poles with the nails at the end you can stick into the ground out in front of your house. You want to see Dwayne down at the Feed and Seed, or stop by Skoglund's yet this evening and pick up yours. I believe that is all that they do on Flag Day, is just fly flags, in Lake Wobegon. I can't really think of what else you could do on Flag Day, though they did use to do more.

It seems to me I heard that back in 1936 about four hundred people in Lake Wobegon put on red, white and blue caps, and they formed what they called a "living flag" out on Main Street. The problem was that there were so many people in the living flag, there weren't many people left over to appreciate it. But they did it. I think it was the idea of a traveling cap salesman who came through town. But Hjalmar Ingqvist more or less organized it. And he didn't see why anybody should have to see it; he thought it was a patriotic thing, and it should be enough for people just to realize that they were a part of the living flag. But as they were standing there on Main Street, of course, somebody broke ranks, and they said, "Excuse me, I'll be right back," and they went and ran up on the roof of the Central Building, right there. And they stood up there and looked down on it, and they said, "Oh, it's beautiful! You ought to see it!"

Part Two

And then, of course, everybody had to have a look. It took hours; one person at a time, leaving the living flag, and running up to the roof of the Central Building up there and looking down at it, and admiring it. And, of course, after a while, the people who'd already had their look were saying, "OK, that's it now, we can go home." And the people who didn't have a look were saying, "Hey, hold on, now. We didn't get our chance!" So every single last one of them had to go up there one at a time. And tempers were running short. And the living flag was becoming sort of a sitting, a kneeling flag.

It was a warm June afternoon. Until finally they came down to Mrs. Quigley, who was the last one. And they said, "All right, go now, Mary. Go now, and make it quick." And she said, "Oh, no," she said, "I don't want you to go to any trouble on my account," she said. "I don't need to." They said, "Go look at it! Go look at the flag, would you now." She said, "Oh, no, I've seen flags before, and I don't need to look at this one." The whole lower right-hand corner of that flag grabbed her and they hustled her up the stairs, and up on the roof of the Central Building, and they leaned her out, and they made her look down at it. And then, of course, somebody thought they would run home and get a camera. So that's why they don't do much for Flag Day anymore in Lake Wobegon, but they will be flying the flag tomorrow.

UNIT 2   A Day at the Circus with Mazumbo

Part One

It was about twelve years ago when those Buehler kids were all little tiny children that the Nobles and Norman Circus came to the ballpark in Lake Wobegon. And they all went to see it, as everybody else did. It was one of those one-ring circuses that travels around under a tent.

When they got done with the circus and they went outside, Ed and the six little kids, and they all got into the old VW, it was like a clown car. I mean all the kids bouncing around and laughing and whooping it up. And Ed pulled out of the parking lot, and there they saw the elephant staked out in the field, old Mazumbo, who'd been in the circus and walked around a couple times and sat on a stool and said her prayers and did some other stuff. And the kids wanted to go feed the elephant.

They said, "Please, Daddy, oh, please, please, please, please. Please can we? Please? We got peanuts," they said. "We got peanuts. Can't we go feed it?" And they did have peanuts. They'd been to the grocery store before the circus. They had about a month's supply of peanuts there and a grocery bag in the back seat. So, Ed said, "All right. But," he said, "you stay in the car." He said, "Nobody gets out of the car. We all stay in the car."

And he drove the VW up right in front of the elephant. They rolled down the window. The oldest Buehler kid took a handful of peanuts and stuck it out for Mazumbo to see. And she put her trunk down there and she picked them up and put them in her mouth. Then it was the next kid's turn to feed her. All six of them. And by the time they got to the sixth handful of peanuts, Mazumbo had quite a bit of her trunk inside the car, feeling around in there and looking around for provisions, which kind of made Ed feel a little queasy because he's always had a fear of snakes. Here was a gigantic long bristly thing snaking around inside the car and looping around people's necks and feeling around on the floor and snuffling and wheezing. And the tip of Mazumbo's trunk looked like Mazumbo had kind of a bad cold. Oh, they just couldn't feed her fast enough. They just stuck fistfuls of peanuts in the end of her trunk.

Then they were out of peanuts. By that time, Mazumbo had almost the whole trunk in there. Ed was trying to keep his calm so as not to frighten the children, but there was no danger of that. Those kids laughing and laughing. Thought that was the funniest thing they had ever seen in their lives. Ed turned around and fished down in the grocery sack for some more food. He felt this huge cold thing on his face. He banged his head on the ceiling. He grabbed Oreos out of there and stuffed it in Mazumbo's trunk. They grabbed candy bars, potato chips, everything he could find. All they had left was canned goods.

And then Mazumbo just kind of lifted her head a little bit. And the left side of the VW went up about two feet.

Part Two

Oh, he could see it then: "Family of Seven Crushed by Elephant. Car Flattened like a Pancake. Investigation Reveals Father Error." He didn't know what to do. He was trying to think: "What do you do? Do you stay with your car? Do you get out and run? What do you do when you've got an elephant's trunk inside your car?"

Finally, he just panicked. He just slipped it into reverse and he backed up kind of slowly because Mazumbo was hanging on by the window. As he inched back, with every inch that he went, he heard the ridges on her trunk go "bonk, bonk, bonk, bonk . . . ." And he was free!

Oh, the kids thought that was the most fun they'd ever had in their lives. All the way home laughing, laughing. They took their arms and put them up to their faces to make trunks and were feeling around and tickling each other, and grabbing onto each other. Oh, they thought that was the best fun.

His little girl in the back seat stood up and put her arms around his neck. She said, "Oh, thank you, Daddy." She said, "You're the best daddy in the whole world." She couldn't see that the sweat was running down the World's Best Daddy's face, and that the World's Best Daddy's hands were shaking so he could hardly drive. The tears were running off his eyes

because it wasn't till right then, you know, that he realized how much he loved them all.

So he could hardly speak until they came up to the driveway. The kids were saying how much fun it was and they couldn't wait to go in and tell Mom about all the fun they had with the elephant. Then the World's Greatest Dad took the long way back around town till they quieted down a little bit and made them all promise that they would not tell Mom about all the fun that they had at the circus, and especially not about the elephant. They all promised. But how could you keep a promise like that? How could you not tell about something as wonderful as that? So, they told her the moment they got in the front door. They told her everything.

UNIT 3   Bruno, the Fishing Dog

Part One

There was an item in the social notes this last Thursday in the *Lake Wobegon Herald-Star*. There was a little item in there that said, "Bob Johnson's dog, Bruno, after visiting at the home of Mrs. Lena Johnson for July and August, will be returning on Friday to his home in Minneapolis." It's not often that a dog gets into the social notes column in the paper, but that dog Bruno is, is an unusual, unusual dog. He is a fishing dog. A dog who has caught fish in the past all by himself. And that's, I guess, why he was visiting in Lake Wobegon July and August, in order to do some fishing down at the lake.

Usually the Bob Johnson family comes up from Minneapolis to visit at Bob's mother's, Lena's, house in town, but they did not come this year. Their visits in the past have been hard, so they only came up for a day. Bob and Merlette came up for about a day in early July to bring their dog, Bruno, up for his summer visit, and then they went back.

So she spent July and August with that dog, that amazing old dog Bruno. He's now, oh, I guess he's about fourteen years old. And that dog, the thing about him was when that dog was about a year old, he was up with the family from Minneapolis. Came up to Lake Wobegon, and was wading around in the shallows just off the beach down by Art's Baits and Night o' Rest Motel. And that dog caught a six-pound walleye! It was right there, and the dog just batted it a couple of times with his paw and grabbed it out between his jaws and ran up to the house. So they made a big fuss over it, and from that point on, that dog became a fishing dog.

Well, he was up there all July and most of August. Go down to the lake every day. Lena let him out the door. Dog go straight down to the lake. Never caught anything. Fourteen years old. That's old for a dog. Doesn't have much longer.

She hated to do it, but she had to take him back to the Cities here this last Friday, as it said in the paper. She was going down for the baptism of her, of another grandchild, Bob and Merlette's little girl, who was born just back in July. So Lena had to put the dog in the car. Dog didn't want to go. She had to grab hold of Bruno's collar and just tow him into the car and put him in. I think he knew that it was his last chance. She drove down to the city.

She got Bruno out of the car. They went for a walk around the streets of South Minneapolis. Old lady, great big dog. She didn't have a leash, didn't know what she would do if that dog bolted and ran away, but he didn't. He walked right at her side, and she talked to him as she had been doing at home for a couple months. She said, "I don't understand them at all. My own children, my own flesh and blood. They move away, and I just don't understand them at all. I can't even believe that they're my own."

So she was late getting to the reception at Bob and Merlette's house. She got the Jello out of the back seat, walked up the front walk toward their huge brick house by the lake in South Minneapolis and walked in. A crowd of people she'd never seen before, all strangers, except for Bob and Merlette, and even them in a way too. Crowded with people.

She went straight back into the kitchen. She was going to put on an apron and help, but there at the sink were two women in white dresses, identical white dresses, who both turned as Lena walked in the kitchen. And they said, "Ma'am?" And she said, "Where's the apron?" She said, "I just going to come and help." She said, "Where's Merlette?" The women said, "Oh, we have everything under control." They were caterers! She'd never heard of such a thing. You have people over to your house, you have somebody else make a meal?

She held out the Jello. She said, "I brought this." They looked at it as if it were not really food. They said, "Well, that's very nice." They said, "We'll just put that in the refrigerator. And if we don't use it today, why, I'm sure Mrs. Johnson will find use for it this week. Thank you very much." She knew she was never going to see that Jello again—a cherry Jello with mandarin oranges and tiny marshmallows in it. She wasn't going to see that put out on the table. No, she was not—because she'd had a look at that table out in the dining room at their buffet dinner. And they had

fresh fruits, and they had vegetables, and they had some kind of cream dip, and they had little things on sticks, and they had little sandwiches. They had everything out there. And they had, in the center of it, they had a huge smoked trout, sitting right there. She knew she was never going to see that Jello again.

She looked and there, through two rooms and out on the other side of a screen door was a familiar face looking in at her. It was Bruno. Thirty feet away, outside that screen door, their eyes met. And that dog looked at her and his eyes said, "Lena, open the door and let me in."

Part Three

And Lena stood up and walked and opened the door. And the dog bolted in past her. She turned and she followed Bruno into the living room where she saw the dog turn and look. And she saw him freeze. And she looked up and saw that his eyes were locked onto that smoked trout. That dog held his position for about a second and a half. She could see that dog was measuring the distance and looking to see if he could get out to the kitchen through the screen door. And then that dog just leaned back on his hind legs, he took about five long leaps and was up on the table. The dog didn't know there was no pad on the table. It was just tablecloth, so when he hit the table, he skidded the length of the dining room table and took everything down on the floor with him. Everything went down, including lighted candles, down onto the carpet. The dog was on top of the wreckage in a moment, got into it, got the fish between his jaws and was gone. And they heard the slap of a screen door.

And in the next second, Lena was down on her knees beside this wreckage, and putting out the candles, and putting them up on the table, and pulling out silverware and straightening things out. She was moving around. She was busy.

She cleaned that whole mess up all by herself and took it into the kitchen. People sat in the living room not knowing what to expect. And then she was there, under the arch. Lena was there, holding out a plate of cherry Jello with mandarin oranges. She said, "Would anybody care for dessert?"

That's the news from Lake Wobegon, Minnesota, where all the women are strong, all the men are good-looking and all the children are above average.

UNIT 4 *Sylvester Krueger's Desk*

Part One

School started, started the Tuesday after Labor Day, as it has in Lake Wobegon forever, going back to when

Adam was a boy, I think, school began on that same Tuesday. My grandfather started school on that Tuesday after Labor Day, my father did, I did when I went to school. All of us on the same day of the year, and all of us in the same old school building in Lake Wobegon. It's almost unchanged in all those years: same desks, same rooms, except for new coats of paint, same floor wax on the floor, that particular kind of floor wax I think they only use in schools, that smell about it, same blackboard, same portraits of Washington and Lincoln up front and center, up over the blackboard: Washington on the left, Lincoln on the right, looking down on us all these years, like an old married couple up there on the wall.

And whenever I was stumped, always look up to see their pictures. Usually looked at Lincoln. He looked more sympathetic, like he might give an answer to a kid, you know. If you looked at him long enough, you might see his lips move. He'd say, "Eight!" Washington looked, I don't know, he looked like he had a headache or something. Mouth was set in that sort of prim line. His eyes were kind of disapproving. I always thought maybe it was because people had made fun of him on account of his hair, which was white and frizzy, like our teacher's, Mrs. Meyer's hair. But she told us that he had bad teeth. So I guess that his teeth hurt. She told us that during dental hygiene class. Was kind of a lesson to us, the father of our country, to brush after every meal and not to eat sweets.

My desk was an antique, ancient was what it was, actually, though I didn't think of it as an antique; it was just what we had, you know. In a town where they don't have a lot of money, you're apt to hold on to things longer, and this one they'd held on to for a long time.

And underneath the desk, there were little lumps of petrified gum, was under there. And names and dates of other kids who had sat at this same desk, because Bill, the janitor, didn't sand underneath it. I remember seeing "CLARENCE 1937" under there, and "JAMES '18." And there was one that was carved in so deeply you could feel it with your fingers, you could read it. It said " '94." Some kid had sat in this same desk in 1894! It was amazing.

Part Two

The most amazing one, though, was a signature which was right up on the top of the desk that said, "SYLVESTER KRUEGER '31," because I found his name also written on the brass plaque that was on the wall by the library door, that said at the top, *"IN MEMORIAM."* And underneath it said, "GREATER LOVE THAN THIS HATH NO MAN THAN THAT HE LAY DOWN HIS LIFE FOR HIS FRIENDS." And underneath there were names, and there was

"SYLVESTER KRUEGER," who died in France in 1944, which made me feel so proud to be sitting in this desk, where this great hero had sat—as great a hero in his own way as Washington or Lincoln. And yet he had been a kid, he had sat in this same desk, and thought the same stuff that I had thought, and did the same school stuff. And I was so proud. I told Mrs. Meyers about it, which was a mistake, because she remembered him, or said she did. She had had him as a student, Sylvester. And she remembered what a good boy he always was, what a good student, and how he never made any trouble. Always was good. And she said, "That gives you a lot to live up to, doesn't it?"

And she'd look at me, and she'd say, "You know, I just might have to move you from that desk." She said, "I don't know that you deserve to sit there." And tears would come to my eyes, for the shame of it, having let down this great hero, who'd sat in this same desk when he was my age so many years ago.

She said it to me one time when somebody put a big gob on the doorknob of the classroom, which Darla Ingqvist touched with her hand. But I didn't do it. She thought I did, because I was the one who laughed the loudest. But if you'd known Darla Ingqvist, you would've known how right it was that she should be the one to put her hand on it, because she was the most stuck-up person in our class. She used to wear better clothes than anybody else ever did. She always bragged about how much money she had in her savings account. And once she brought a ten-dollar bill to school to show off to people.

So it was exciting that day when she was the classroom monitor so she had the privilege of opening the classroom door. And to watch, knowing what was on the doorknob, watch her reach for it, and then see her yank her hand back after she knew what was on it.

Part Three

And I was punished for it. I was sent to the cloakroom, even though I hadn't done it. But she let me sit in that desk, right through the end of the year, sit in Sylvester Krueger's desk. And I remember that toward the end of that year, I think it was around Arbor Day, we had a ceremony in the schoolyard, and we planted a tree in memory of Sylvester and all of the other boys who died for freedom. Darla Ingqvist was the one who got to read the Gettysburg Address. She was chosen for that, and then we put the tree in its hole, and we tapped down the dirt around it. Just a little sliver of a tree, didn't even have any leaves on it, didn't look like it would last long, even though we watered it every day. And it didn't last long either, because we had put it out in deep left center field of our softball diamond. And so even before the school year was out, it got stomped on by somebody during the baseball game at the all-school picnic, a game in which, by the way, I hit a double. And it was a real double. It was a clean double, went right down the right field line. And it would have been a triple, except I tripped. So life goes on. And that's the news from Lake Wobegon, Minnesota, where all the women are strong, all the men are good-looking and all the children are above average.

UNIT 5   The Lake Wobegon Cave

Part One

They were working on the pig barn there at the Tolleruds'—Daryl, the old man, and Carl—and the five Norwegian bachelor farmers watching them. And then the Tollerud children came home. And—what's the youngest boy's name? Paul, I think—came and sat down on the sawhorse next to Mr. Haugen. I think it was Mr. Haugen.

And Mr. Haugen said, "Well, Paul," he said, "how are you doing?"

Paul said, "Oh, all right."

He said, "Paul," he said, "Uh, did you know that there's a cave down just over the hill here on your Grandpa's property? Oh, yeah." He said, "Your Great-grandpa Tollerud, uh, discovered that, uh, cave back, uh—oh, when was that?—it was about, uh, 75 years ago."

And he told him about it. This is an old story. The Lake Wobegon Cave. Nobody has seen it in 75 years, but Great-grandpa Tollerud was missing his pigs one March afternoon. And he went out in search of them. They'd broken through the fence and he went over the hill and down into the woods and there, in the big rocks just below the oak tree, he saw it was a cave in there. And he heard pig grunts coming out of there. And he crawled down about 15–20 feet of cave, and he came to a big room full of blue light. There were some of the pigs wandering around in the cave. They'd gone down there to get warm.

And he called them, "Here, piggy, piggy, piggy, piggy." But most of them didn't come. He got a few of them out, but most of them went farther back. He followed them a little ways and there were stalactites and stalagmites, almost—real sharp ones like skewers you might put pigs on—but the pigs running around in there, and wandering farther and farther back in this cave.

And so he got a few out, and he left the rest in there. And then he blocked up the entrance to the cave so the children wouldn't go in there.

Mr. Haugen told the little Tollerud boy all this. He said, "Ya, that's the story about that cave. Your Great-grandpa discovered that when he lost his pigs down there."

Part Two

The boy said, "What happened to the pigs?"

He said, "Well," he said, "they're still there." He said, "You go out in the woods, uh, anywhere, in fact, even in town. You put your ear down to the ground and you can hear them down there. Sometimes, usually late at night, you can hear them down there, 'Grunt, grunt, grunt, grunt, grunt.' They're down there, but there are quite a few more of them than there used to be."

The boy said, "How big do they get?"

"Well, it's hard to say. Uh, the one that I saw was, uh, was pretty big, about the size of an elephant, actually. But it was, uh, dark out. See, their eyes are used to the dark down there, so they only come out at night. They never come out during the day."

"But, but how can they get out if they blocked up the entrance to the cave?"

"Well, you see, it's a big cave. It runs for miles, this cave does. It runs under the ground, under town, and all around here." He said, "It's a great big cave and those pigs are good diggers, you know. They've got those two big long curved tusks, and you've seen pigs root around in the dirt. Well, they dig their way up. You see, they are trying to get up, out of the cave. And they usually try to get out through a basement because then they don't have quite as far to go, you see. They're down there under the ground and they can smell bacon frying and so they head for that smell of bacon frying," he said, "and they head for the basement." He said, "Tell me," he said, "Paul," he said, "you got, you ever go down in your basement? You got cracks in the floor of your basement?" He said, "Is there a place down there where the floor is kind of bulged up? Ya, I thought so. That's, uh, where a big pig is down there pushing up with his shoulders trying to get out."

The boy said, "Do, do many of them get out?"

"No," he said, "I, I haven't heard of too many that get out. The bigger ones, mainly, are the ones that, uh, get out, but, uh," he said, "you," he said, "you can, uh, sometimes ward them away by going down in the basement and jumping up and down and yelling." He said, "Does your dad ever do that? Does he ever go down into the basement, down there by himself, jump up and down and go 'Ay, ya, jits, ah, cha!'?"

"Ya," the boy said. "Ya."

"That's what he's doing. He's scaring away those pigs." He said, "Uh, you ever hear creaks in the house at night?"

The boy said, "Ya."

"Ya, those are pigs. They're getting closer. They are pushing up with their shoulders."

The boy said, "How do they breathe down there?"

He said, "Did you ever go down in your basement and you smell a real rotten smell down there? That's pig breath. It's pig breath."

The boy turned to Daryl and he said, "Dad, is that true?"

Daryl looked at Mr. Haugen. Mr. Haugen winked at him. Daryl thought about the time when he heard that story about thirty years ago. He didn't go in the woods for two weeks.

He said, "Dad, is that true?"

"No," Carl said, "It's not true. Not a word of it."

Mr. Haugen said, "Now wait a minute, Carl. There's more to this than that."

Carl said, "It's not true," he said, "I'm going home. See you tomorrow."

"OK," they said. "OK, then. You go home. Don't stop on the way."

That's the news from Lake Wobegon, Minnesota, where all the women are strong, and all the men are good-looking and all the children are above average.

UNIT 6 Thanksgiving: The Exiles Return

Part One

Well, it's been a quiet week in Lake Wobegon, Minnesota, my old hometown. Holiday this last week and the return of the exiles, come back to their home. Children grown up and moved away, had families, learned how to complicate their lives in all sorts of new and interesting ways, come back every year to a little town so much the same it's hard to look at it and not believe you're still twelve years old. And that's how some of the returning children behaved too. They came back.

A lot of them drive up from the Cities with their families and they make a last stop at the Crossroads Lounge about ten miles down the road. As they come up over the rise and down into town, the last drags are taken on a lot of last cigarettes, and the first of a lot of breath mints are popped into their mouths.

But the returning children were not the only ones trying to get things shined up. I tell you, it was a week of intense housekeeping in Lake Wobegon. A lot of homes that had gotten along on tuna fish casserole and meat loaf and hamburger hot dish were doing some pretty fancy cooking here this last week.

They had hors d'oeuvres at the Tollefsons' for Thanksgiving. Hors d'oeuvres, if you can believe it! It was just little weiners on sticks, a little liverwurst and Ritz crackers, but food on the coffee table had never been seen in that home before. And their dog was kind of surprised by it. Figured it was for him. Had a little bit of it, but of course it wasn't. It was for Claudia and for her husband, Todd, who drove up from Chicago, where they are quite active in the arts. Mom and Dad wanted to do what was right by them.

Virginia Ingqvist, for the turkey this year, tried out a new recipe, one that involved deboning the turkey breast and peeling back the skin and making kind of a dressing pâté and scooching it under the skin and then pulling the skin back over it and wrapping string around this thing, which she had seen a woman do on *Good Morning, America* in about 45 seconds flat with a couple of little twists of the knife.

But it was a harrowing experience for Virginia! When she got done with it, her hair was hanging down around her face, and she was cursing under her breath. The turkey looked like it had been in a head-on collision with something. Put it in the oven, squirted some juice at it from time to time, and took a later look and it had all fallen apart and just lying there in a big heap. It wouldn't have been recognizable to its closest friends.

Part Two

But she's a valiant woman. She pulled it out of there, whacked that meat apart, tossed it in a casserole dish, dumped a little cream in it and a little sherry—whatever spices were close at hand—tossed in some flour and squeezed an orange into it, threw it back into the oven, cooked it for another hour, brought it out and served it in bowls.

At the Bunsen home, they finished their turkey, cooked the regular way. So Barbara Ann, Arlene cleared off the dinner, worked on it in the kitchen, worked at the wreckage. Barbara Ann was just as glad that nobody else had offered to help. It had been a long time since she had been alone with her mother in a kitchen, kitchen where they had spent so many hours together over the years. Working together, you know, with your hands busy in the kitchen, you can say a lot of things that you might not be able to say to each other at the table. If you said it at the table, it would be too blunt, it'd be too dramatic. Everybody would stare at you. When you can work around in the kitchen, there's kind of a close silence there around you, working at things. And without looking at someone, just make a little announcement, like, "I'd like to go to Chicago. I need to borrow some money." Or, "I went to see the doctor last week." There's a little announcement you make. Or, "Am I good-looking? Am I smart?" And more than once her mother, over the years, working, hands in the dishwater, without looking up or anything, just said, "I want you to know how proud we are of you." It's better if it is said in the kitchen, you see, just release these little sentences out into the air.

Well, Barbara Ann dried the dishes. Her mother washed. They got to doing the dishes and her mother started to sing. And as they sang and did the dishes, Barbara Ann was surprised to find that she still knew where everything went. The platter went up on top of the refrigerator. The sieve nested in the mixing bowls down to the left of the sink. And the gravy boat went up behind the cereal boxes. And the little centerpiece, the little plaster Pilgrims standing by their plaster cabin with the plaster pine tree and the plaster smoke coming out of the chimney, was wiped off with a damp cloth and put away in the china cabinet until next year.

That's the news from Lake Wobegon, Minnesota, where all the women are strong, all the men are good-looking and all the children are above average.

UNIT 7 Father Emil's Starry Night

Part One

Now, there was a salesman come through town, I believe it was on Wednesday. He came through in a crimson Cadillac sedan. Turned everyone's head. And he was selling satellite TV dishes.

Father Emil was interested. He heard about it, latched onto this salesman, wanted to hear about it. Father Emil was thinking that maybe real good reception in the Youth Center in the church basement might attract more of the young people than have been coming in lately to read the fine literature. And he was thinking maybe charging them a quarter a head, maybe fifty cents for a feature film, you know he could pay it off in about a year. But then the salesman showed him the brochure that described the channels, and the programs that you'd get with a satellite TV dish. And he kind of skimmed over a few pages real fast, and he sort of put his hand over some of the photographs. And Father Emil got an idea that there might be some programs coming across with that TV dish you wouldn't want to get a good sharp reception of. And so he said no.

He's always been kinda leery of television. It's so strange. He doesn't have one himself. And when he's looked at it, everything is so odd; the people are odd. They're all young, or if they're old, they're funny, or they have gas pains. Old people are kind of ridiculous on television. It almost never snows on television. There's almost no cloudy, overcast days. Television isn't made in Minnesota, evidently; comes from someplace else. And the people in the commercials are so odd.

How excited they get about a new detergent, or a cup of coffee; it's as if they're impoverished, as if they've been in solitary confinement for years, so that they get this particular bottle of pop and they just go bananas over it.

Father Emil's brother came out from Dallas to visit him about three years ago, offered to buy him a television set for the rectory. He said, "I say, I don't know how you can live like this, what you do without one." He said, "I don't know how you live in a place like Lake Wobegon, for that matter." He said, "I sure know I couldn't." Father Emil just looked at him. He said, "I would have made a good monk." And he did.

At one time when he was eighteen years old. Father Emil was eighteen in 1931, when his father sold their farm out in western North Dakota. It was 1931. His father had always had bad luck farming. And he only got enough for the farm to buy a truck. His father was tall and thin and sallow and had a sad face and empty eyes, so that you almost could not bear to look into his eyes. He almost never spoke. He was a silent man who brooded about his bad luck.

And on this night, the day before they were to go west to California, Emil helped his father load the furniture, except for the mattresses, into the truck. It was dark. There were stars out, millions of stars outside the tiny white house, out in flat, flat country, no trees around. He and his father stood there after they had loaded the truck, and his father offered him a cigarette. And they stood and smoked. And Emil felt that at last his father was about to talk to him.

Part Two

And after a while, his father cleared his throat and he said, "It's about time to make something of yourself, about time you started out on your own, I think." Emil said, "I thought I was going with you!" His father said, "It's time to make something of yourself." So he left that night. He slept in fields and he hitchhiked for three days to reach the monastery. And when he got there, they took him in, and they gave him a room and they gave him food to eat. And for the first time in his life, he felt as if God loved him, and so he became one of them. He awoke every morning to hear the monks singing, off somewhere, a beautiful song, and knew that he was loved. And at night, was so happy that he would walk for miles by himself, which he still does, goes walking at night, when it's not too cold, as he did the other night, when he pulled on his sweater, and his big black topcoat, and his stocking cap, and set off down the street. It was about nine o'clock, walking along in that gait that all Catholic children in Lake Wobegon have been able to recognize since they were tiny. A slight limp, so when he walks, it's almost like a waltz. He goes, "ttch, TTCH, ttch, TTCH, ttch, TTCH, ttch,

TTCH." Not that fast, that's downhill. Walking down the street, looking at the houses, the stars shining high above, beyond the branches. The houses shining too, some of them, with a little bluish television light, as children sit and lean towards the television and watch attractive men and women talk. Men and women who are more attractive for being behind the veil of very poor reception. Attractive men and women talk and an audience laughs someplace, and these children laugh, then too. Sit and stare at attractive men and women who really do not care about these children, cannot care about them. And the one who does is walking down the street, who they might not even notice if they saw him, but who walks by every house, and as he walks by, says to himself the names of everyone who is inside, which of course, he knows, and which is a sort of blessing: "Know that you are loved, little children."

UNIT 8   Storm Home

Part One

Well, it has been a quiet week in Lake Wobegon, my hometown. Though there were a few moments here this last week. I think back to this last Tuesday when the Hochstetters had to come in off the farm, come in to town. Rollie needed a new belt for his woodsaw. And they were only gone into town about two or three hours. But when they got back home, they found about sixteen chickens and ducks and geese strewn out down the snow, down in between the hen house and the toolshed, with their throats ripped open, lying there, all bloody in the snow. And all the other livestock upset, even the Holsteins, who looked like they'd been to a horror show, and wanted to jump over the fence and into somebody's arms. They figured that a pack of wild dogs did it. Rollie found dog tracks around where the bodies lay. And some of the neighbors had seen packs of big dogs out in the woods, roaming around. It certainly was a caution to people to realize that the countryside was not so peaceful as it appeared, and especially was a caution to some of those children who live out there near the Hochstetters' and go to Sunnyside School, which is just west of Rollie's. And it certainly is a lot on a person's mind if you are eight years old and you walk half a mile twice a day in dim light, early morning and late afternoon, down a road into the woods, and the woods are dark, and you know that there are wild dogs out there. And you can almost hear them breathing. It's scary, even when there are older children with you, and in fact, especially when there are older children, because it's the older children who like to talk about it as you are walking down the road, and who say things like, "It'd be about those dogs' breakfast time right now. I'll bet they're real hungry right now. They can smell food a long ways away, four or five miles away. And they run so fast, you never even see them when they come at you." And you're a little kid and you walk a little faster.

I tell you, when I get scared now, one way that I have of quieting myself down is to think back to when I went into the seventh grade, and so didn't go to Sunnyside School anymore, but caught the school bus into town to go to Lake Wobegon High School. And Mr. Dettman was the principal then, and though it was September, he was already thinking ahead to winter and to the blizzards that we had every year. And on the first day of school, each of us children who rode the bus in from the country was handed a little slip of paper that said, "Your storm home is . . . ." and then it said. And we were each of us assigned to someone's home in town, where if a blizzard came during the school day, they wouldn't try and ship us home on the buses, but we'd go to our storm home, and spend the night there.

Part Two

Mine was the Kruegers. My storm home was the Kruegers, an old couple, back then, who lived in a little green cottage. It was down by the lake. And I can see it now because I walked past it so many times, looking at my storm home over the years. It was a beautiful green cottage. And everything was so arranged about it, and so neat and so delicate.

It was the kind of house that if you were a child and were lost in a dark forest, and you came across it in a clearing, you would know that there was a kindly old couple living there who would take you in and rescue you, and that you were a lucky child who had gotten into a story with a happy ending. They became very big in my imagination, Mr. and Mrs. Krueger. And there were many times I walked by their house, and I felt like introducing myself to them. I felt like saying, "I'm the kid who if there's a blizzard, I'll come and stay with you." You see, because we seemed to have some relationship in the world.

I often dreamed of going to see them when things got hard. Blizzards aren't the only storms, you know, and not necessarily the worst thing that can happen to a child. And I often dreamed about going and knocking on their door. And she'd open the door, and she'd day, "Oh! It's you. I knew you'd come someday. I'm so glad to see you. Won't you come on in, and get out of those wet clothes? Come on into the kitchen, sit down, I'll make you some chocolate. Would you like an oatmeal cookie or something?" She'd say, "Oh, it's terrible outside, isn't it?" I'd say, "Yes." She'd say, "It's going to get worse, they say." "Yes, it probably is." She'd say, "Carl, come on down here, see what's in the kitchen!" He'd say, "Is it our storm child?" She'd say, "Yes! He's sitting here, in the flesh, big as life!" We'd play cards, we'd go up to bed or something.

I never did go there. We didn't have any blizzards that came during the day that year or the year after that. They were all convenient blizzards—evening, weekend blizzards. But they became a big part of my imagination. And I always thought that I could go to the Kruegers'. And I didn't, I guess, because all of my troubles were bearable troubles, but I'm certain that they were more bearable for imagining that the Kruegers were there, my storm home, and that I could go see them. Whenever things got bad, I think, "Well, there's always the Kruegers."

UNIT 9 Starting the Car in Winter

Part One

It's a matter of pride, up here, to have a car that starts in the coldest weather. It's something people are so proud of that sometimes they lie about it.

It's true of Carl Krepsbach, though, back home. It's always been true. Even on bitterly, bitterly cold mornings, he goes out to his garage, and he gets in his old Chevy, and he pumps the gas pedal about eight or ten times. And he just talks to it a little bit, turns the key—she jumps right up. Starts right up, big roar every morning, even if it's forty below, forty-five below zero, his car starts every morning. It's a sound, the roar of that engine, that has been depressing his brother-in-law, Lyle, who lives next door for years now; Lyle Janske, I mean, Carl's brother-in-law. Sitting there in the kitchen, he can hear Carl's car start right up. Lyle's car is not trustworthy anywhere below freezing. And when it's colder than ten below, there's even no point in trying. And Lyle's car is an old Chevy, too, which leaves just one variable in the equation, and that's Lyle.

And then the worst of it is that Carl always comes over to help Lyle start his. And sometimes he doesn't even need to use jumper cables. Sometimes he just reaches in under the hood, and he just fiddles with something in the carburetor. And then Carl gets behind the wheel of Lyle's old Chevy, turns the key and she starts right up. That's the maddening part: when you've got an insoluble problem, an impossible problem, and some cheerful person reaches over your shoulder and says, "Here, why don't you try this?" And Carl's cheerfulness is pretty hard to take, too, when it's gotten down to thirty-some below.

Lyle is the science teacher up at the high school. He can explain cold; he just can't accept it, because he was born, and grew up, and spent most of his life in Southern California. He's lived in Lake Wobegon now for almost ten years, but some of these transplants don't take, you know. Some of these Southerners who move up to the North, their tissues reject winter. And when it first snows, even after ten years, Lyle looks out the window and he says, "What's wrong? What is that stuff?" And when it gets down to thirty-some below at night, Lyle thinks, "This is not right. It's not supposed to be like this." And then his brother-in-law, "Cool Carl," comes over in his big parka, and his big boots, and a big smile on his face, and he says, "Boy, she's a cold one today! Boy, I think she must be thirty-some below out there!" Lyle'd just like to shoot him!

So I think it was Monday morning, Lyle woke up. It was cold in his bedroom. So cold in bed even his wife felt chilly to him. She's from Minnesota. Lyle kind of thinks that her temperature drops during the winter, like bears, you know. He got out of bed, ran into the bathroom to take a hot shower, turned on the water, nothing came out. Felt terrible. Put on his clothes. That didn't make him feel much better. Went down to make some coffee, and about the time the coffee was just starting to perk, he heard the roar of Carl's car. He knew that Carl always goes back into the house and leaves the old Chevy warm up. Lyle knew he had about fifteen minutes.

Part Two

He put on his coat, went out to the garage. He was just praying, "Lord, let it be today." Got in behind the wheel, turned the key. It gave out that horrible moan, "haawwwn." He knew he had about ten minutes left. He was desperate. He didn't want to be helped again, and that was why he went and got that whole bag of charcoal, and put it in the garbage can lid, and lit it. And when he got some good coals going, he shoved it under the engine, and went in the house to warm up.

Carl is also the captain of the volunteer fire department. He was the one who made the call. He was the first one on the scene. The truck came. Everybody came. You kind of think of a car fire as being like in the movies, you know, a big fireball, which maybe was what Lyle wanted. But this one just smoldered, and it gave off a stench that you could smell all over town. The fire department came barreling up, the siren going. Everybody came from blocks around. They said, "How'd it happen?" Firemen didn't know how to answer that with Lyle standing there. Kind of hard to explain, but there was the answer, sitting right there on the floor, garbage can lid, hot coals in it. People thought, "That man is teaching our children about science!" He didn't know how to explain. He didn't have any idea something as cold as his car would be combustible. They hauled it out of the garage, managed to save the garage. The car is going to need quite a bit of work. And Carl put his arm around Lyle, and he smiled at him, and he said, "You should have called me up. I would have come over and helped you! What are brother-in-laws for?"

UNIT 10 Ella Anderson's Sunset Years

Part One

Ella Anderson was out, uh, cleaning out her flower bed here on Monday, it was. About the first time she's been seen outdoors since back on Thanksgiving. Old woman with her bad hip. She can't navigate on the snow, on the ice, so she stays indoors. And then, of course, after three, four months of being cooped up inside, she's a little bit stiff in the joints, so she has to kind of start slowly in spring training and, uh, bring herself along a little bit. She moves very slowly out there around those flower beds.

And this year is trying out a new stand-up technique of gardening because she's afraid that if she got down on her knees that she might not be able to get back up again, which is a frightening thought for her, to think about that. Not so much that it would be painful, but the fact that if nobody were there, she'd have to wait for someone to come down the street, someone she barely knows, and then she'd have to call for help. She hates the thought of that: calling out to somebody for help, you know.

It's lonely there in the house, being cooped up with Henry month after month after month. It's not that he's such bad company after all these years, but sometimes he goes out of his mind. And not that that's necessarily bad either. Henry looks up from the couch where he lies and looks at the window and he says, "Where are we now? What town are we going through?" And in his mind, he's riding the *Burlington Zephyr* from Chicago to Saint Paul. And that's when Ella's mind has to be very sharp.

She has to go to the window and look out. And she can't just say, "Oh, there's, uh, a field out there, and uh, the river over there, and looks like we're coming into a town." He wants to know what's in the field and exactly what town it is. And if she gets the stops out of order, or skips a town—if she says, "Oh, we're coming into Pepin now, dear," he'll say, "What? You didn't wake me up when we went through Fountain City!" because even when his mind is gone, he still remembers that route exactly. So she says, "Oh, no, dear, this is Fountain City. Yes, I see this is Fountain City that we're coming

into." And he says, "Oh, yes, it does. It looks like Fountain City. I should have recognized it myself, dear. Beautiful town."

She's the only one who can give Henry this trip. You see, if their daughter Charlotte were there and Henry said, "Where are we now? What town are we going through?" Charlotte would panic. She would want to call a doctor. It would be an emergency to her. But to Ella, Charlotte's faith in doctors is made of the same stuff as Henry's train trip.

Part Two

Ella would like to have more visitors. She kind of keeps the window open for Henry, you see, on Wisconsin 1917. She'd like somebody to keep the window open for her on Minnesota 1984, and come and tell her stuff as she tells Henry things and have people come and visit her.

And that was why she put up the sign in her flower bed on Monday, written in large letters, Magic Marker on cardboard box, that was stuck onto a picket and hammered into the ground. My, it took her a long time to do that! And the sign said, "Visitors Welcome. Free Coffee. Come In."

Charlotte had a fit when she heard about it. The neighbors called her. Oh, Charlotte was angry! She said, "How could you do this to me?" She said to her mother on the phone, she said, "You're just trying to embarrass me, make me look like a fool in front of people." She said, "I come see you as often as I can. I do everything I can, that I possibly can for you. Now go out and take that sign down. Please take it down, Mother!"

Well, Charlotte takes everything so personal. Fifty-five years old, she is, and worried sick about her own health. She'd drive two, three hundred miles to go see any specialist that she's heard about, reciting to herself all the way, rehearsing her list of symptoms, her speech that she'll make. They are as familiar to Ella, Charlotte's symptoms are, as all the stops of the *Burlington Zephyr*.

She would just like to have some visitors. "Visitors Welcome. Free Coffee. Come In." And you wouldn't have to stay a long time. And you wouldn't have to say an awful lot. And you wouldn't necessarily have to tell the truth either, because loneliness is so dramatic it makes all of your problems seem so big and tragic, which hers are not. Hers are fairly normal old lady problems. And they would seem more ordinary, you see, if there were someone there to talk to, if there were a friend there. It just would seem more natural and ordinary. You could even talk about death as if it were normal and something that happens to many people. You could turn to your friend and you could say, "I'm ready. I think I'm about ready to go." And the friend might say, "That's good." And then you'd look up and you'd see that the friend is Death. And you'd say, "Oh, dear, I think my legs fell asleep. Give us a hand here. Help us up." And Death would say, "Yes, that's all right. Here you go."

UNIT 11 Uncle Ed, the Norwegian Bachelor Farmer

Part One

I think about the Tollefson girl, Tina, who moved down to the city. She came down here and went to college, married a boy who sat next to her in psychology class, to whom she always gave the answers. Gave him enough good ones so that he got into law school. Got on with a good law firm, they bought a nice house out by Lake Harriet in Minneapolis, started having children. That was about twenty years ago, twenty-some years ago. Some of the children already grown up and moved out; just have one left. So that when her mother wrote to her about two weeks ago, and said, "Your Uncle Ed has to come down for an operation Monday next, but it would be more convenient for me if I could bring him down on Friday. Could you put up with him for a couple of days?" she said, "Of course." So down he came.

Her Uncle Ed is one of what we call Norwegian Bachelor Farmers. Old, old man. Lives in a two-room house just west of town. Farms about eighty acres with the help of a couple of big black Belgian horses, named Queenie and Gus. Raises wheat, mainly. Lives by himself. Keeps his place fairly neat, according to his own standards. Keeps himself fairly clean, according to the same. Splashes on a little wintergreen every week or so. Whenever he feels uncomfortable being with himself, he takes a bath.

Well, she decided she'd take him out for a night on the town in a city he'd never seen. Her husband said, "Oh, I think he'd be a lot happier just staying here in the house with us." And she said, "Maybe so, but he's never seen a city before. And I would feel if I kept him here that maybe part of it was because I was ashamed to be seen with him. So we're going to take him downtown." And they got in the car. She sat in the back seat with Uncle Ed. They drove around the lakes. He was kind of curious about people running around the lakes. What were they doing? She said, "They're doing that for exercise, Uncle Ed." He said, "That's kind of dumb, ain't it? Why don't they get work? Why don't they get jobs?"

They went downtown. They took him to a restaurant at a hotel. They walked in, the maitre d' looked at them,

looked at this old man in the old suit, with his work boots on, his hair not combed, looked at the well-dressed couple and their well-dressed son. Maitre d' thought, "Well, that's their business."

Part Two

He gave them a table back in the corner, back behind a palm tree. Uncle Ed is hard of hearing. When he talks, his voice carries, all the way to the kitchen. The waiter brought him a brandy, which he had asked for. Uncle Ed looked at it. He picked out the ice cubes. "Goddamn," he said, "charge you two bucks for a drink, and then they water it down." He picked out the ice cubes. Tina's husband was looking off at the ceiling, he was looking off at the walls, as if he didn't know these people, they'd just come in, they'd been seated at his table, he was not with them. This was not happening. The boy sat there grinning. He'd never seen his dad so embarrassed. He wanted to see more of it. Tina, she sat by her uncle, and she talked. She carried on a monologue. And when people at other tables kind of snuck a stare over at them, she looked right back at them, she stared right back at them, as if there was nothing wrong.

And when they got up, she went with him to the salad bar. And when he said, "Goddamn, they sure give you small plates, don't they?" She said, "Yes, they do!" And when he heaped it all up with the macaroni salad, she paid no attention. And when the waiter brought him the broiled torsk with a sauce on it, and Uncle Ed took a bite of it, and he said, "That's a hell of a shame to do that to a fish!" she just kept on talking. She just kept on talking about the family and all the people that she remembered from when she was young, and the people that come over from Norway, and all about their history.

Well, he went in for the operation on Monday. They let him out on Friday. The doctors said six months or a year, they didn't know how long. But then again, with somebody like Uncle Ed there's no telling. They drove him home to the farm. The horses were there waiting for him, Queenie and Gus. They hadn't eaten all week. The horses, they knew something was wrong. They'd been standing all week out behind the barn, looking for him off down the road. The car came in the yard, and they saw he was in it, and they called to him. And he managed to walk over there and get out a couple ears of corn, and a pail of oats, and a forkful of hay, and put it down for them. And he spoke to them in Norwegian, the only language those horses understand. And he told them that the city was a hellhole, but some of the people in it weren't bad, and he was glad to be back, and he was tired, and he was going to go in and lay down and take a nap, and tomorrow they would go out and cultivate. And that's the news from Lake Wobegon, Minnesota, where all the women are strong, all the men are good-looking, all the children will be above average.

UNIT 12 Mr. Turnblad Makes his Dream Come True

Part One

Lake Wobegon's produced a lot of dreamers up there. The one I was thinking about today is Mr. Turnblad, whom I knew as a boy, who built an ocean-going yacht in his potato barn. Been more than twenty-five years ago. He, uh, farmed out north of town. I always just thought of him, you know, as the little guy in overalls who rode on the Farm-All pulling the digger as it went up and down the rows of potatoes, and dug them, and us kids followed along behind dragging the gunny sacks and, and picking them. Kind of associate him with hot August days and September and dirt in your mouth and the gunny sack getting heavier and heavier. I had just always thought of him that way, as the man who would circle around and yell at me to keep up with the others.

But evidently, Mr. Turnblad didn't think of himself the same way. He thought of himself as a man of the sea, even though he had never seen it in his life. He thought of himself as, as a captain who lacked but two things: just a boat and an ocean.

Evidently, he was a secret reader all his life of books on sailing and those adventure books by Richard Haliburton and the Horatio Hornblower books and, uh, *Two Years Before the Mast* by Richard Henry Dana. And he just read those books all of his life and imagined himself at the helm in heavy swells. And maybe sometimes when he rode on the Farm-All as it kind of pitched up and down going over the potato rows, maybe he thought he was on a boat. And maybe he imagined that the dust that came up from the field was the spray from the ocean.

But one year there was lumber in the potato barn. There was cedar lumber and there was oak that he was making some kind of frame from. And then the year after that when we went to pick potatoes, there was a sort of a hull out there in the potato barn, which we didn't know was a hull. We just assumed it was a storage bin for potatoes, and we filled it almost completely up until we heard it crack, which was the first time I ever saw a grown man cry. He didn't even yell at us. He just leaned against it, put his head in the crook of his arm. And he just stood there and wept.

But the next year he had rebuilt it. And then the year after that there was sort of a deck on it, and it started to look like a boat. And then the year after that I didn't work for him anymore. I went to college, which was kind of my dream. And I was happy to get away from picking potatoes. And I imagine that he was too.

The year after that it was a May morning when the flatbed truck came, and they hauled that boat out of the potato barn. They had to tear down the potato barn to get it out, but that didn't bother Mr. Turnblad. He didn't intend to ever see it again. Kind of bothered his son Wilmer, who was taking over the farm. Matter of fact, all the Turnblad children were kind of upset about it. They were afraid their dad was never going to come back. But the truth was he didn't intend to.

Part Two

Well, he made it to New Orleans by September. And he headed out into the Gulf of Mexico. He'd gotten the rigging up by then. Headed out to the Gulf for his first sailing lesson with a manual on sailing nailed to the helm, reading it as he went.

And evidently, he learned something from that manual because he made it to the coast of Florida. And he went on down to the Keys, and he settled there, in Marathon in the Florida Keys. And first thing, he had a picture taken of himself to send back home to his children. And I saw it, and it wasn't the Mr. Turnblad that we knew. It was a different man. He was wearing a white captain's hat. He was wearing big black shades. He was standing there in the cockpit of his boat, and he had his shirt off. He was awfully lean and muscular. And I'll tell you, the Mr. Turnblad we knew never took his shirt, never would have taken his shirt off, any more than he'd take off his pants. But here he was: without his shirt on and with one foot up on the rail, and looking into the camera. And those dark glasses seemed to say, "You don't really know me at all." And that smile on his face said, "Don't expect me back anytime soon."

He went into the charter business there in the Florida Keys, took people out fishing, mainly. And came back only once, for Wilmer's funeral. Wilmer died young. Wilmer died of a heart attack out in the field one summer. He came back for that but didn't stay. He went right back down to Florida.

And though I think he thought about going farther, maybe going to the Bahamas or going to England, something about the Atlantic told him he'd gone far enough. He'd used up a lot of his luck by then. And he was over seventy. And also, if you have spent your whole life raising potatoes, you don't have to get an awful long way away from land to feel like your curiosity has been satisfied. So he stayed there.

Answer Key

UNIT 1   The Living Flag

2 Listening

A. 2. f   3. g   4. i   5. b   6. h   7. a   8. e   9. d

B. (Answers will vary.) It is a flag made of people. Everyone puts on a red, white or blue cap and stands together to form the United States flag.

C. 2. c   3. b   4. a   5. c   6. b

D. 1. b   2. a   3. c   4. a   5. b   6. a   7. b   8. c
9. c   10. b   11. c

F. 1. b   2. b   3. c

3 Getting the Joke

1. a   2. b   3. c

4 Reviewing Vocabulary

2. caps   3. patriotic   4. leftover   5. broke ranks
6. have a look   7. tempers were running short
8. that's it   9. Hold on   10. were kneeling (knelt)
11. make it quick   12. lower right-hand   13. hustled
14. lean

8 Getting into the Language

B. 3. don't make   4. buy   5. have   6. work
7. Have, gotten   8. to do
9. had (is having, is going to have)   10. printed
11. got (is getting, is going to get)   12. to buy
13. won't make (aren't going to make)   14. wait
15. have   16. processed   17. have   18. sent

UNIT 2   A Day at the Circus with Mazumbo

2 Listening

A1. 2. nose   3. hairy and rough
4. sick to their stomachs   5. in cans
6. supermarket   7. VW   8. provisions

A2. 1. d   2. a   3. e   4. c   5. b   6. f   7. g

B. (Answers will vary.) They began feeding Mazumbo all of the food they had in their grocery sack, except the canned goods.

C. 2. T   3. F   4. F   5. F   6. F   7. F   8. T
9. F   10. F

D. 1. c   2. a   3. a   4. c   5. b   6. b   7. b   8. c
9. c   10. b

F. 1. F   2. T   3. T   4. T   5. T   6. F

3 Getting the Joke

1. c   2. c   3. c   4. c

4 Reviewing Vocabulary

1. staked   2. were out of   3. fished down
4. canned goods   5. were whooping it up (whooped it up)
6. feel queasy   7. crush   8. pulled out (was pulling out)
9. quiet down   10. tickled   11. keep their promise

8 Getting into the Language

B. (Answers will vary.)
1. b. Two people were injured in a car accident that happened over the weekend
c. John Ewing won the 800-meter race at Lake Wobegon High School.
d. The city is investigating the delays in the construction of the hospital.
e. The chairman of the hospital, Mr. (Ms., Miss, Mrs.) Bunsen will (is going to) address the City Council on Tuesday.
f. The Minneapolis Museum bought a Van Gogh (a Van Gogh painting) for three and a half million dollars.
2. b. New Hospital Rules Raise Costs
c. Yankees Win Against Twins in Opening Game of Series
d. State Studies New Plan for Capital Subway
e. 20 Trapped in Highrise Elevator
f. Damaged Plane Lands Safely at Municipal Airport in Fog

UNIT 3   Bruno, the Fishing Dog

2 Listening

A. 1. c   2. a   3. e   4. b   5. f   6. g   7. h   8. d

B. (Answers will vary.) When he was about a year old, he caught a six-pound walleye.

C. 1. T   2. F   3. F   4. T

D1. 1. h   2. b   3. g   4. a   5. d   6. k   7. f   8. i
9. c   10. j   11. e

D2. 1. c 2. a 3. b 4. c 5. b 6. a

E. (Answers will vary.) She felt uncomfortable; she felt like a stranger.

F. 1. T 2. T 3. T 4. T 5. T 6. F 7. T 8. F 9. F 10. T

G. 1. i 2. g 3. a 4. j 5. f 6. b 7. e 8. c 9. k 10. h 11. d 12. l

I. 1. c 2. a 3. b 4. c 5. b

3 Getting the Joke

1. b 2. c 3. b 4. a 5. c

4 Reviewing Vocabulary

1. was wading (waded) 2. made a fuss over
3. straight 4. reception 5. flesh and blood
6. caterers 7. froze 8. bolted 9. leap 10. skidded
11. straighten things out 12. under control
13. care for

8 Getting into the Language

B. 2. P-H 3. P-H 4. F-P 5. P-H 6. F-P 7. F-P

UNIT 4 *Sylvester Krueger's Desk*

2 Listening

A1. 1. c 2. g 3. h 4. a 5. d 6. b 7. l 8. f
9. j 10. i 11. k 12. e

A2. 1. c 2. a 3. b 4. c 5. a 6. c

B. (Answers will vary.) He found names and dates carved in the wood.

C. 1. F 2. T 3. F 4. T 5. F 6. T 7. T

D. 1. h 2. f 3. a 4. j 5. b 6. g 7. d 8. e
9. i 10. c

E. (Answers will vary.) She might move him to another desk.

F. 1. c 2. a 3. b 4. c 5. b 6. a 7. c

G. 1. c 2. j 3. e 4. f 5. a 6. h 7. g 8. b
9. i 10. d

I. 1. T 2. F 3. T 4. F 5. F 6. T 7. F
8. F

3 Getting the Joke

1. b 2. c 3. a 4. c 5. b

4 Reviewing Vocabulary

1. portraits 2. stumped 3. be apt to

4. had made fun of (made fun of) 5. held on to
6. carved 7. brass plaque 8. live up to 9. let down
10. stuck-up 11. bragged about 12. was out

8 Getting into the Language

B. 1. Having monitored the all-school picnic yesterday, today I need a long rest.
2. Having been in school all winter, the children were very excited to be playing outside.
3. Yesterday, watching the children play softball, I worried the whole time about our little tree.
4. Then, however, moving back to catch a ball, a boy stomped on the tree and broke it.
5. Afterwards, I cut off the rest of the tree, remembering my old student Sylvester Krueger.

UNIT 5 *The Lake Wobegon Cave*

2 Listening

A. 1. f 2. k 3. g 4. j 5. e 6. c 7. i 8. b
9. d 10. h 11. a

B. (Answers will vary.) Great-grandpa Tollerud went looking for his pigs and discovered some of them in the cave.

C. 1. F 2. T 3. F 4. T 5. F 6. T 7. T
8. F

D1. 1. f 2. b 3. e 4. a 5. g 6. d 7. c

D2. 1. a 2. b 3. c 4. b 5. c 6. a

F. 1. a 2. c 3. b 4. c 5. a 6. b

3 Getting the Joke

1. c 2. b 3. a 4. c

4 Reviewing Vocabulary

1. was missing 2. property 3. ran 4. crawled
5. were wandering around 6. blocked up
7. It's hard to say 8. creaks 9. rotten
10. scare away 11. winked

8 Getting into the Language

B1. (Answers will vary.) Mr. Haugen exclaimed that he had seen one the size of an elephant. Then Paul asked if the pigs ever got out of the cave. Mr. Haugen answered that some were still there but that some had gotten out. Paul then wanted to know how they had escaped. Mr. Haugen replied that they had pushed up through somebody's basement.

B2. (Answers will vary.) Paul said, "Yes, I do."
Then Mr. Haugen said, "The creaks are signs of the pigs."
Paul asked, "How can the pigs breathe in the cave?"
Mr. Haugen answered, "The rotten smell in your basement is caused by pig breath."
Paul asked his father, Daryl, "Is the story true?"
Carl answered, "No, it isn't."

UNIT 6   Thanksgiving: The Exiles Return

2 Listening

A1. 1. b   2. c   3. a   4. b   5. c   6. b   7. a

A2. 1. k   2. f   3. d   4. c   5. g   6. a   7. j   8. b
9. e   10. l   11. i   12. h

A3. 2. i   3. c   4. a   5. h   6. b   7. f   8. e   9. g

B. (Answers will vary.) Housekeeping (cleaning) and cooking.

C. 1. c   2. b   3. a   4. b   5. a   6. c

D1. 1. c   2. c   3. a   4. b   5. b   6. a   7. a   8. b
9. c   10. a

D2. 2. g   3. d   4. b   5. a   6. c   7. f

F. 1. b   2. a   3. b   4. c   5. a   6. c   7. b

3 Getting the Joke

1. b   2. a   3. b   4. b   5. c   6. c   7. b   8. b

4 Reviewing Vocabulary

1. shined up   2. had gotten along on (got along on)
3. hors d'oeuvres   4. tried out   5. flat   6. harrowing
7. valiant   8. close at hand
9. was cursing under her breath (cursed under her breath)
10. was just as glad   11. went   12. wiped off

8 Getting into the Language

B1. Barbara Ann was just as glad that nobody else had offered to help. It had been a long time since she had been alone with her mother in a kitchen, the kitchen where they had spent so many hours together over the years.

B2a. 1. had told
2. had been prepared

B2b. 1. had warned
2. had not expected
3. had not had
4. had been fixed

UNIT 7   Father Emil's Starry Night

2 Listening

A1. 1. f   2. c   3. a   4. g   5. b   6. d   7. i   8. e
9. j   10. h

A2. 1. a   2. b   3. c   4. c   5. a   6. b   7. a   8. c

B. (Answers will vary.)
1. He thought about buying a satellite TV dish for the church Youth Center.
2. There were some programs available on satellite TV that were not appropriate for young people to watch.

C. 1. c   2. c   3. b   4. a   5. b   6. a   7. b   8. c
9. c

D. 1. b   2. d   3. e   4. f   5. c   6. a   7. i   8. j
9. k   10. g   11. h

F. 1. F   2. T   3. T   4. F   5. F   6. T   7. T
8. F

3 Getting the Joke

1. b   2. c   3. b   4. a

4 Reviewing Vocabulary

1. latched on to   2. pay off   3. skimmed   4. leery of
5. odd   6. go bananas   7. monk   8. brooded   9. bear
10. was starting out   11. it was about time
12. make something of himself

8 Getting into the Language

B. 2. has spoken   3. preached   4. made   5. thought
6. discovered   7. put   8. turned   9. went
10. has not said   11. has been thinking

UNIT 8   Storm Home

2 Listening

A. 1. c   2. h   3. k   4. g   5. f   6. d   7. b   8. i
9. a   10. j   11. e   12. l

B. (Answers will vary.) A storm home is a family home where a student can wait during a blizzard. Storm homes are assigned to students who live in the countryside but who go to school in town.

C. 1. a, b   2. a, b, d   3. b, c, d   4. a, b

D. 1. d   2. e   3. g   4. c   5. b   6. a   7. f

F. 1. a, b, c, d   2. c, d   3. a, b, d   4. b

3 Getting the Joke

1. c   2. b   3. a   4. c

4 Reviewing Vocabulary

1. strewn   2. came across   3. ripped open   4. figured
5. roaming   6. livestock   7. dim   8. blizzard
9. felt like   10. would rescue (were going to rescue)
11. bearable

8 Getting into the Language

B1. (Answers will vary.)
   b. If we did not have troubles, we would not need storm homes.
   c. Some children in Lake Wobegon might not look forward to blizzards if they did not have storm homes to go to.
   d. If the Kruegers did not live in town, they could not be (eligible to be) "storm parents."
   e. Mrs. Krueger might not sign up for the storm home program if she had children of her own.
   f. If Mrs. Krueger liked packaged oatmeal cookies, she would buy them.

UNIT 9   Starting the Car in Winter

2 Listening

A1. 1. m   2. b   3. d   4. a   5. l   6. g   7. e   8. j
   9. c   10. f   11. i   12. k   13. h

A2. 1. b   2. a   3. c   4. b   5. c   6. a   7. c

B. (Answers will vary.)
   1. His car starts even in the coldest weather.
   2. He worries that he will not be able to start his car.

C. 1. c   2. b   3. b   4. a   5. c

D. 1. c   2. j   3. f   4. i   5. a   6. e   7. d   8. b
   9. g   10. h

F. 1. b   2. c   3. c   4. b   5. a

3 Getting the Joke

1. a   2. b   3. c   4. a   5. c   6. b

4 Reviewing Vocabulary

1. bitterly   2. there is no point in   3. transplant
4. depresses   5. parka   6. maddening
7. is hard to take   8. moan   9. lid   10. coals
11. shoved   12. was smoldering   13. stench
14. hauled   15. combustible

8 Getting into the Language

B1. b. should have put
   c. shouldn't have gone

   d. should have drunk
   e. should have noticed
   f. shouldn't have left

B2. b. Perhaps if I had put less charcoal in the garbage can lid, the fire I made wouldn't have been too hot.
   c. I imagine that if I hadn't gone inside to warm up, I would have been able to watch the coals closely.
   d. If I had drunk only one cup of coffee, not two, the fire wouldn't have had a chance to spread.
   e. If I had noticed the stench coming from the fire earlier, I would have had a chance to call the fire department myself.
   f. If I hadn't left the coffee pot on the stove while the fire department was here, I wouldn't have burned the pot and Carl wouldn't have offered me a new one so cheerfully.

UNIT 10   Ella Anderson's Sunset Years

2 Listening

A. 1. d   2. e   3. k   4. c   5. f   6. j   7. i   8. g
   9. b   10. h   11. a

B. (Answers will vary.) She helps him take imaginary train trips.

C. 1. b   2. c   3. a   4. b   5. c

D. 1. d   2. g   3. c   4. h   5. f   6. b   7. e   8. a

F. 1. c   2. c   3. c   4. b   5. b   6. c

3 Getting the Joke

1. a   2. c   3. b   4. b

4 Reviewing Vocabulary

1. flower bed   2. had been cooped up   3. bad company
4. skipping   5. out of order   6. worried sick
7. symptoms   8. specialists   9. had a fit
10. look like a fool

8 Getting into the Language

B1. 2. should have consulted   3. could have called
   4. could have avoided   5. must have thought

UNIT 11   Uncle Ed, the Norwegian Bachelor Farmer

A. 1. b   2. f   3. a   4. c   5. d   6. e   7. i   8. j
   9. g   10. h

B. (Answers will vary.)
1. He had to come to the city to have an operation.
2. She decided to take him out because he had never seen the city. She also wanted to prove to herself that she was not ashamed to be seen with him.

C. 1. a   2. c   3. b   4. c   5. a   6. b   7. c   8. a

D1. 1. d   2. c   3. g   4. h   5. f   6. i   7. e   8. b
9. a

D2. 1. b   2. a   3. c   4. b   5. a   6. c   7. a   8. c

F. 1. b   2. a   3. b   4. c   5. c   6. b   7. c   8. a
9. a   10. b   11. c   12. c

3 Getting the Joke

1. c   2. b   3. a   4. b   5. a

4 Reviewing Vocabulary

1. put up with   2. a night on the town   3. ashamed
4. was hard of hearing   5. kept on
6. that's their business   7. carried on (was carrying on)
8. grin   9. shame   10. there was no telling
11. take a nap

8 Getting into the Language

B. 1. went   2. gave   3. had had   4. took   5. felt
6. stared   7. had been   8. was   9. said
10. had said

UNIT 12   *Mr. Turnblad Makes His Dream Come True*

2 Listening

A1. 1. f   2. a   3. e   4. i   5. d   6. h   7. c   8. g
9. b

A2. 1. b   2. a   3. c   4. a   5. b   6. c

B. (Answers will vary.)
1. He dreamed of becoming a sea captain.
2. He built a boat and sailed away.

C. 1. b   2. b   3. a   4. c   5. c   6. a   7. b   8. c

D. 1. a   2. a   3. b   4. b   5. c   6. c   7. b

F. 1. c   2. b   3. c   4. b   5. b   6. c

3 Getting the Joke

1. b   2. c   3. c

4 Reviewing Vocabulary

1. thought of himself as   2. ocean-going yacht
3. tore down   4. was taking over (was going to take over)

5. Evidently   6. assumed   7. manual   8. settled
9. lean and muscular   10. chartering

8 Getting into the Language

B1. b. Mr. Turnblad was a potato farmer who built an ocean-going yacht in his barn.
c. He thought of himself as a captain who lacked a boat and an ocean.
d. Mr. Turnblad was a great reader whose favorite books were adventure stories.
e. The people (whom) (that) Mr. Turnblad had hired to pick potatoes could not distinguish between a hull of a boat and a storage bin for potatoes.
f. The boat (that) Mr. Turnblad built was almost as large as the potato barn.

B2. b. By September, Mr. Turnblad had made it to New Orleans, which is a port on the Gulf of Mexico.
c. The boat, whose every feature was known to Mr. Turnblad, must have been seaworthy, since he continued sailing it to the Florida Keys.
d. Mr. Turnblad, who usually avoided having his photograph taken, sent his family a snapshot of himself from Florida.
e. The photograph, which was taken by a friend, showed Mr. Turnblad in a white captain's hat, shades and no shirt.
f. Wilmer, whom everybody loved, died of a heart attack.
g. Mr. Turnblad, whose original dream had been to cross the Atlantic, later decided not to sail beyond the Florida Keys.